BEYOND
SUFFERING

Ten Women Who Overcame

CAROLYN CHESNUTT

RELIANT
PUBLISHING
A DIVISION OF REDEMPTION PRESS

BEYOND SUFFERING

Ten Women Who Overcame

Published by Reliant Publishing, an imprint of Redemption Press, PO Box 427, Enumclaw, WA 98022

Toll-Free (844) 2REDEEM (273-3336)

Redemption Press is honored to present this title in partnership with the author. The views expressed or implied in this work are those of the author. Redemption Press provides our imprint seal representing design excellence, creative content, and high quality production.

The information of several of the women listed were gathered from various sources, such as television interviews, articles, and other types of media. These sources were not quoted directly.

All Scripture quotations, unless otherwise indicated, are taken from the Holy Bible, New International Version®. NIV®. Copyright © 1973, 1978, 1984 by International Bible Society. Used by permission of Zondervan. All rights reserved.

Bible references marked NASB are taken from the New American Standard Version of the Bible. Copyright © 1960,1962,1963,1968,1971,1972,1973,1975,1977,1995 by The Lockman Foundation. Used by permission.

ISBN: 978-1-68314-567-7 (Paperback)
978-1-68314-568-4 (ePub)
978-1-68314-569-1 (Mobi)

Library of Congress Catalog Card Number: 2018937242

Dedication

This book is dedicated to my mother,
whose unconditional love, forgiveness,
wisdom, and strength of character
greatly blessed all who knew her.

Contents

Acknowledgments

I would like to thank my publisher, Athena Dean, and my editor, Inger Logelin, of Redemption Press, for their encouragement, enthusiasm, and very wise advice. This book never would have been published without their help.

Deep gratitude goes to my late father, Dr. David Wyatt Aiken, and my sweet mother, June Rose Roepe Aiken, for letting me live with them during the six years it took to research and write this book. They were very easy to love and a joy to care for in their eighties. I will always be indebted to them for their Christian example and the love they showered on me my whole life. My mother was a patient listener to many of my chapters. My dad went to heaven when he was ninety before the book was in a readable form.

Special thanks to my sister, Susan Fonger, for her excellent advice and encouragement. Being a writer herself, she understands the demanding work that writing can be.

I want to thank Ruth and Val Canon and Cindy Aston for always being available for advice and comfort. Many thanks to my daughter, Caroline Chesnutt, and her friends for reading the book and expressing the benefits it brought to them. Also many thanks to the friends who prayed for me through this work and who all encouraged me to keep going. My daughter Catherine Henry's anointed prayers, wisdom, and inspiration were invaluable.

Heartfelt thanks to my life coach, Susan Rome, and to my counselor, Barbara Porch, for their wisdom, knowledge, understanding, and direction, and to Lanier Grimm, who has been a faithful and supportive friend for many years and a great blessing in my life.

Exceptional thanks go to Patricia Strachan of New Orleans who sat through hours of my reading her the chapters. She was always attentive and sweet and said she really liked the book. I am also very grateful to Cindy Aston and Karen Mase for their faithful friendship and support.

Thanks to Sherry Bell and her love of history. Her suggestions and appreciation have been invaluable. And thanks to Arlene Grimm for her encouragement and vision.

My prayers are being lifted up for Carole Ross of Cross Prison Ministries in Gatesville, Texas. Without her prayers, the Holy Spirit might not have anointed this book.

But of course, the greatest thanks goes to God for His faithfulness to these women and His faithfulness to me. May all the glory of our lives be given to Him. He is so kind, so gracious, so real, and so wonderful. Thank You, heavenly Father, for this book.

Introduction

Jesus suffered out of love for us and obedience to His Father. He paid for our sins with His blood, dying on the cross. He rose again from the dead to ensure for us eternal life if we trust Him, believe in Him, and make Him our LORD and Savior. A   friend once told me she had forgotten that suffering is a part of the Christian life. No one wants to suffer. Even Jesus in Gethsemane asked His Father to let the cup of suffering pass Him by.

If we are past elementary-school age, we have all suffered in various ways. I wanted to write a book about the women whose lives encouraged and inspired me while I was going through hard times. I never meant to write about suffering. But when the book was almost finished, it became clear that all the women I was profiling suffered greatly. My editor pointed out that this book is about overcoming suffering; so we titled it *Beyond Suffering:*

Ten Women Who Overcame.

Two of these women, Sabina Wurmbrand and Elisabeth Elliot, I knew in person, so I could ask them questions. Sabina and Elisabeth were both already well known when I met them. They were humble enough and patient enough to answer my elementary questions. I was totally blessed to have known them.

This book is the result of my years of research, which included talking to Sabina and Elisabeth, reading their writings, reading others' writing about them, and researching others.

God wants to heal us. He wants to comfort us in our suffering. He wants us to get beyond suffering. Yes, we will sometimes still be hurt, but God does not want us to live in the problem but in the solution, which is Jesus Christ Himself.

While facing hard times, I would often think of these women I knew about who had gone before me and who had suffered more than I had. These are women who knew Jesus as their personal Savior and served Him with their lives and in their families. From Sabina Wurmbrand, who went to a slave-labor camp for Him, to Susanna Wesley, who with great difficulties raised her children to know Him, to Madame Guyon, who went to prison for her deep, intimate prayer life and devotion to God, these women became my mentors. I studied their lives and read all I could find about them. They were a blessing to me. All that I had to suffer seemed insignificant compared to what they suffered. Thinking about their perseverance and endurance helped me through times of heartache and loneliness. Someday when I am with my Savior in heaven, I hope to meet them and talk to them about their lives and learn more about what God did for and through them.

I have always been inspired by the faithfulness and determination of Saint Augustine's mother, Monica. She prayed for her son for at least eighteen years, following him from city to city in Italy, crying continually and begging God to turn her son back to Him. God honored her and answered her prayers.

I also loved Adrienne de Lafayette, Madame Guyon, and Hannah Whitall Smith. I wish I could sit with each of them for hours and hear about their relationships with God. One of the reasons I look forward to heaven is the hope of meeting them and hearing their stories. Our contemporaries, Miss Kay Robertson and Sonya Carson, are truly models of gracious achievement.

There are many more women who have been an inspiration to me, but I centered on a few of the strongest. I hope that they will increase and encourage your faith, hope, and love.

There are discussion questions at the end of each chapter so the book can be used in a Bible study or Sunday school class. Some of the chapters are very short and can be combined into one study.

My hope and my prayers are that as you read this book, you will enjoy it and learn more about God and His love for us. I hope you will see the faithfulness of God as He blesses His special daughters through their trials and sufferings. They all suffered a great deal, but they overcame, and so can we. I hope that you will also be inspired and encouraged by the beauty of their lives.

Jesus told us that "in this world you will have trouble, but take heart, I have overcome the world" (John 16:33). May we be inspired by their stories to overcome whatever troubles we have, just as they have done.

One

Sabina Wurmbrand: Tortured for Christ

The guards in the hard-labor camp picked up Sabina Wurmbrand, held her by one arm and one leg, and heaved her into the rocky canal the women in the prison camp had been working on. She thought she had broken a number of ribs, but since there was no medical care available in the prison, she could not be sure. She had been teaching Bible studies and praying with the women in her dormitory, so the guards wanted to make an example of her. They wanted to show the other women what would happen to them if they kept up their religious activities.

Sabina Wurmbrand was imprisoned and tortured by the Communists in Romania for her faith in Jesus Christ in the 1950s before the fall of the Communist regime. She was the godly, devoted wife of Pastor Richard Wurmbrand and served with him in ministering to the underground church in Romania for years.

While her husband was in prison, Sabina organized the women and the few Christians left who were not in prison. She carried on ministry, just as she had worked beside her husband for so many years. The Communists told her that if she would renounce her faith, they would let him go. She refused. They then told her that if she would give them names of other Christians, they would set him free. Again, she refused.

Richard Wurmbrand spoke warmly and openly about God's faithfulness to him in prison when he stayed with us in Dallas, Texas, for a week. At one point he had tuberculosis, and his captors thought he would surely die. Years later, after his release, Richard told me and my family that his lungs were as riddled as cheesecloth. So they put him in the "dying room," where those who had no hope were kept until they left this earth. For three years he lay there telling everyone who was placed in the room about the saving love of Jesus Christ. He said the room became a gateway to the entrance of heaven. Men would be brought in, find the peace, love, and forgiveness of Jesus, and be ushered into eternal life by all the believers in the room.

During this time, Sabina Wurmbrand worked quietly in the background. She dressed like a peasant, wore a babushka on her head, and carried on the work of the ministry that she and her husband had done together. Her husband had written numerous books, which they sold at their appearances. She had written one, *The Pastor's Wife*,[1] telling her story.

Sabina made sure to let her husband shine, always putting him first. I thought her book was better than his, but of course I never told Pastor Wurmbrand that. I loved both of them very much. Her English was also better than his, and she was an excellent speaker, but she never spoke in public if he was present. People may find this old-fashioned, but Sabina and Richard shared a wonderful mutual admiration and love. He adored her and introduced her whenever he spoke: "I would like you to meet my *beautiful* wife." He could never have achieved what he did without her.

When the Communists took over Romania after World War II, they quickly enslaved the country, forcing people to submit to them or suffer the consequences. They gathered the religious leaders in an auditorium. Sabina and Richard Wurmbrand were both Christian leaders and were included in the gathering. One by one, the pastors went to the microphone and stated that Communism and Christianity were compatible. They agreed to become state churches and comply with whatever the Communist regime ordered them to do.

[1] Sabina Wurmbrand, *The Pastor's Wife* (Bartlesville, Oklahoma: Living Sacrifice Book Company, 1970).

Sabina sat with her husband and encouraged him to go forward and speak the truth about true Christianity and Communism. They listened with dismay as one after another religious leader capitulated. They knew enough about Communism and its effects on the Christian churches in other countries to know that the Communist leaders were not telling the truth. Finally Sabina urged Richard to go up and take a stand for Jesus Christ. Jesus's teaching, they both knew, was in direct opposition to the teachings and practices of Communism.

"If I go," he warned, "you will no longer have a husband."

She answered bravely, "I don't want a coward for a husband."

Pastor Wurmbrand went forward, took the microphone, and began speaking about Jesus Christ. He explained that Communism teaches that religion is a crutch and an opiate of the people. Wurmbrand preached that Jesus Christ must always come first in our hearts and lives, and that Communism or any other political philosophy must bow to the truth of Jesus.

Quickly the Communists in charge ran up, cut the cord of the microphone, and hustled Pastor Wurmbrand out of the assembly. Sabina and Richard Wurmbrand continued ministering to the underground church, but they knew that their days of freedom were numbered.

Sabina was born July 10, 1913, into a Jewish family in Czernowitz, a city in the Austro-Hungarian Empire in what is now the Ukraine. During World War II, Romania was occupied, and Sabina's parents, two sisters, and one brother died in Nazi concentration camps.

Sabina had studied languages at the Sorbonne in Paris and was studying law when she met and married Richard Wurmbrand at age twenty-three. He was proud of his wife and used to brag that she was a lawyer. He was also Jewish, and they were very much in love.

In their first year of marriage, Richard came down with tuberculosis and was sent to the mountains of Romania to recuperate. There they were converted by a devout Christian man, and both of their lives changed dramatically. Having accepted Jesus Christ as their Savior, Richard gave up his job as a stockbroker and Sabina stopped her work as a lawyer. They began working in the underground church. The Wurmbrands spent the first twelve years of their marriage rescuing Jewish children from ghettos, teaching in bomb shelters, and being arrested for underground Christian activities. With the end of World War II came thousands of Russian troops and severe Communist control. The Wurmbrands expanded their underground activities. Sabina witnessed to the Russian soldiers, organized camps for religious leaders, and conducted street meetings with gatherings of up to five thousand people.

With their underground work, Sabina and Richard both knew they could end up in prison or lose their lives. Richard purposefully read *Lives of the Saints*, studying those who had endured torture, preparing himself for the worst.

In 1948, Pastor Wurmbrand was denounced by a traitorous friend, arrested, and sent to prison. Sabina cared for their young son and carried on the work of the ministry without her beloved Richard.

Pastor Wurmbrand suffered for fourteen years in prison, three years in solitary confinement. Sabina herself was sent to a hard labor camp for three years.

Sabina said that when the Christian men were sent to prison, the women simply took up the ministry. Almost all the pastors and leaders had been incarcerated by the Communists, leaving a vacuum of leadership. The women did not sit around and discuss theologically whether they were doctrinally correct in filling the vacuum. The need was there in the body of Christ, so the women filled the need.

The Communists did not expect the women to be so strong and keep the underground church going, according to Sabina,[2] so after three years they rounded up the Christian women as well and put them in prisons and hard-labor camps.

[2] Sabina Wurmbrand, *The Pastor's Wife* (Bartlesville, Oklahoma: Living Sacrifice Book Company, 1970).

Sabina was put in a slave-labor camp with other religious women and political prisoners who were persecuted by the Communists in Romania in the 1940s. In prison, she taught Bible studies and ministered to the women as best she could, and the guards knew it. They didn't like it. At the first opportunity, the guards held her by one arm and one leg and threw her into the canal the women were filling with rocks.

She thought she broke a rib and fractured other bones, but since no medical care was available in the camp, she did not know. She kept on ministering, urging women to trust Jesus and love God and follow His ways.

Sabina worked with hundreds of other women in the slave-labor camp, where they had to break up rocks and throw them into a canal. The rocks tore their clothes and made them look like rags. The women missed their children and wondered how they were surviving with no parents—some of the children living on the streets. The women were beaten, and their faces were usually streaked with dirt, blood, and tears.[3] One night she was enclosed, as punishment, standing in a box with nails sticking out from the sides aimed at her body. She could not relax or the nails would press into her skin. She was left in the stand-up box all night. She said that she could not have made it through the

[3] Wurmbrand, *The Pastor's Wife*.

night if she had not prayed the whole time in her prayer language.

Sabina continued her Christian ministry. She led the women in secret Bible studies and prayer meetings in the prison dorms. One night they lay on the cement under a bed so that the guards would not see them. She said it was like paradise being together. With no printed Bible allowed, they took turns reciting Scriptures they had memorized. One woman had memorized the sixth chapter of Acts, telling of the stoning of Stephen, the first Christian martyr. The Bible says his face shone like an angel as they stoned him to death.

This story made a great impression on a lady who had been very wealthy. Her husband had been imprisoned because he was the political leader of the opposition party to the Communists. She asked what beauty parlor Stephen had gone to. Sabina explained to her that Stephen had not gone to a beauty parlor but that his faith in Jesus Christ gave him an inner joy which radiated outward. This woman accepted Jesus as her Savior, and her face shone like an angel's face there in the prison.

Sabina and Richard both talked about the pain of never seeing children, colors, green grass, or trees while in prison. The women missed their own children immeasurably. Once they were told if they did a certain amount of work, they would be able to see their children, but only with guards watching and only for ten minutes. They worked very hard. Sabina planned for days what she would say to Mikael, their son. When she finally faced him, he looked so frail and weak that she forgot all she had planned to say and was speechless. He also had planned many speeches but when he saw his mother in rags, beaten down, dirty, her face smeared with blood, he forgot everything he had planned to tell her. Soon the guards took him away, and desperate to give him her best, she shouted out, "Mikael, love Jesus with all your heart!"

When Sabina was released from prison, she found her son to be a committed Christian, ready to fight for the kingdom of God. He came to America with his parents and did a great deal of work helping refugees.

After Sabina was released from prison, she still had to live in poverty and under house arrest for a number of years. While Richard was still in prison, the authorities repeatedly told her that if she would give up her faith and renounce Jesus, they would release her husband. She refused. Then they told her that he had died. She refused to believe them. A man who was released from the same prison that her husband was in told her that he had heard him preach through the wooden walls of his cell. Although he was in solitary confinement, Pastor Wurmbrand knew prisoners were being taken down the hall outside his room, even though they had to wear socks so as not to make any noise. So The Pastor, as he was lovingly called in Romania, preached in a loud voice through the walls so that the other prisoners could hear him. He preached about the love of God and the saving power of Jesus Christ.

He was released in 1964. In 1965, the Wurmbrands and their son were ransomed from the Romanian government for $10,000 by a group of Christians in Sweden. If there were one word to describe the Wurmbrands' living epistle, it would be *forgiveness*. They prayed for their enemies, held no bitterness, resentment, or unforgiveness towards their captors, and prayed for their salvation.

The Wurmbrands traveled through England after leaving Sweden and arrived in the United States. Pastor Wurmbrand testified in the US Senate hearings, telling the world of the horrors of the treatment of Christians and others by the Communists. He took off his shirt and showed TV audiences the scars on his back where he had been cruelly whipped.

Sabina helped Richard start the ministry the Voice of the Martyrs to alert the world to the plight of persecuted believers around the world, but always they preached forgiveness. Sabina and Richard worked together in this ministry until Sabina went to her eternal reward in 2000. Richard followed his wife to heaven two years later. Their work continues through the Voice of the Martyrs. Their message is sometimes not popular. It is hard for people living so comfortably in America to think about Christians who are suffering physically, financially, emotionally, and psychologically in other parts of the world.

The Wurmbrands traveled throughout the United States, telling their stories, preaching the gospel, and asking Christians to "Remember the prisoners, as though in prison with them, and those who are ill-treated, since you yourselves also are in the body" (Heb. 13:3 NASB).

Sabina preached by her life that it is an honor to suffer for Christ, that it was her choice and her privilege. Sabina and Richard could easily have obtained their freedom by renouncing their faith. But they did not, could not, and would not deny their beloved Lord and Savior, Jesus Christ. And God used their suffering in their ministries to help those who are still suffering for Christ.

Getting Personal

When my husband filed for divorce in 2010, I experienced great emotional suffering. I went to live with my parents in New Orleans, Louisiana. For one year all I could do was walk in Audubon Park, pray, and go to Bible studies. I couldn't work, could hardly function, and felt like my life was over. I have heard that the greater the loss, the greater the grief. My loss was great, as was my grief. Grief is something that simply must be experienced and worked through.

I wanted to be healed and to be able to live life to the fullest. I found a Christian book on healing. It said that the first thing you must do to be healed is to have no blame. That means we cannot blame God, blame ourselves, or blame others for what we are suffering. Many people believe they are doing the right thing even when they hurt other people. Most people are doing the best they can, and hurts sometimes just happen. I am sure my husband thought he was making the best decision he could at the time he filed for divorce, so I do not blame him. I stopped blaming myself for the failure of our marriage, and if I ever blamed God, I stopped that too.

I had a lot of anger that I was not aware of during this time. I have heard that anger turned inward can cause depression. I definitely suffered from depression. I endured all the negative emotions that accompany grief from divorce or loss of a loved one. Anger, depression, guilt, loneliness, and many other symptoms of grief were hard to endure. I was not even aware of my anger until a friend pointed out that she heard anger in my voice. I cried a lot. I had to pray a lot and work through the emotions to be set free from my anger. Praying for those who had hurt me helped me work through

my anger. Praying about my situation and asking
God for guidance and healing definitely helped.
Reading Scripture and studying the Bible helped
me.

Forgiveness came next. Forgiveness is a decision of the will and a process. It is not a feeling.
It often requires ongoing work. Sabina's example
of forgiveness helped me to forgive. She had suffered so much more than I had, and she forgave
and prayed for her captors. Surely I could forgive
my husband and those who had encouraged him
to divorce me and marry someone else. My heart
was broken, but healing required total forgiveness
from my heart.

Getting to know the Wurmbrands

After graduating from Dallas Theological Seminary in Dallas, Texas, my then-husband had run
for office in our district so that he could serve God
in politics. I began visiting gatherings of people to
help him build support. Looking through our local
newspaper, I saw a picture of the clenched hands
from the cover of *Tortured for Christ*, written by
Pastor Richard Wurmbrand. Pastor Wurmbrand
and his wife, Sabina, were going to visit a church
in our area, and I was thrilled to take my children
to hear them.

I had first heard about the Wurmbrands from
my mother. My mom had been impressed by Pas-

tor Wurmbrand's suffering for Christ in Communist Romania, and she had given many copies of his book, *Tortured for Christ*, to family and friends. The cover of the book showed two hands handcuffed and raised in agony. I had not read it, because I did not want to read about human suffering. But when Pastor Wurmbrand came to speak at the church near us, I had the glorious opportunity of meeting Sabina Wurmbrand.

Sabina was warm and welcoming and talked personally with each one of my children. She signed my Bible at Psalm 34, one of her favorites. There were very few people in the church, and Sabina spent a long time with us. I believe she wrote in our children's Bibles as well. She and Richard both loved children and made ours feel very special.

While we were waiting to hear the Wurmbrands, our oldest daughter, Christy, asked if she could go forward in the church to tell Richard hello. Of course I agreed, so she went up to introduce herself. He took her upon his lap and held her until he got up to preach. She was about eight years old and was thrilled with the attention.

I did not know when we met Sabina in Dallas that she and her husband would later be staying with my parents in New Orleans for a week to speak at churches, Bible studies, and Sunday school classes. Shortly after I met her, I was able to go and stay with them and help with their visit to my parents' house in New Orleans, Louisiana.

Later the Wurmbrands stayed with our family for a week in Dallas while they spoke at churches and Bible studies. Having the Wurmbrands stay in our home for a week was a great blessing for our family. We loved being with them. They were so humble, so loving, and so kind. One night after dinner, Pastor Wurmbrand gave us all communion, and he personally gave the bread to each of our children. I have a picture of that evening that I treasure. They required a private bedroom and bath and no visitors and we were glad to accommodate them. After every meal, Pastor Wurmbrand said he needed to rest and would go to their room. Sabina would smile and indicate to us that he was not really resting. We understood that he went to commune with God. They were both totally immersed in the reality and presence of God, always ready to minister and let God's love flow through them.

While they were staying with us in Dallas, they spoke at churches and Bible studies. Pastor Criswell of the First Baptist Church of Dallas was open to Pastor Wurmbrand's message. He said "Yes!" when I asked if Pastor Wurmbrand could speak. Before they came, I had seven months to prepare for their visit, but I doubted I could get ready in time. The Lord encouraged me through His Word: "Do not be afraid any longer, but go on speaking and do not be silent; for I am with you, and no man will attack you in order to harm you, for I have many people in this city (Acts 18:9–10 NASB). So I began calling and asking, calling and asking. Many doors were closed, but those God had arranged beforehand opened. This illustrates Ephesians 2:10: "For we are His workmanship, created in Christ Jesus for good works, which God prepared beforehand, that we should walk in them" (NASB).

When Sabina was with us in Dallas, I was amazed at how mild mannered, kind, and quiet she was. She was the main support of her more famous husband, and she was used by God as marvelously as her husband.

They were both so forgiving, loving, and humble. I learned a great deal about forgiveness from them, and their example helped me to forgive any who had hurt me. Remembering Sabina's kind and tender ways helped me.

When the Wurmbrands were staying with us, my husband was in awe of all that Pastor Wurmbrand had been through and asked Richard to explain the purpose of suffering. Pastor Wurmbrand said, "You are asking the wrong question. It is as if you are asking, 'What is the melody of a peach?'"

We tried to think of different ways to ask the question, but we were stumped. He would not elaborate or give any of the routine answers as to why bad things happen to good people. My husband kept pressing Pastor Wurmbrand. Finally he turned to us as if he were giving away top-secret classified information and declared, "Cheap love is worthless."

That ended the conversation. What could we say to this couple who had suffered so much that the power of God emanated from them? Their love was not worthless.

Sabina was much easier for me to understand and to relate to than her enigmatic husband. Her simplicity, devotion, love, and kindness deeply moved me. I will never forget her. She has gone to heaven now, but her suffering for Christ inspired me and helps me to endure the small trials God blesses me with.

Once when my then-husband and I struggled financially, I remembered Sabina and her courage and patience while suffering. It made my trials easier to bear. My life was so much easier than hers had been physically, so how could I complain? Once while I was disciplining the children and trying to teach them to do the right things, I became angry and frustrated. The memory of Sabina's sweetness, kindness, and long suffering helped me to regain control. She had a great calming effect on me.

Let's Talk

1. What do you know about the persecution of Christians in other parts of the world ministered to by Voice of the Martyrs?
2. Does anything in your own life relate to what Sabina suffered?
3. Why do you believe God allows suffering in the Christian life?
4. Can you think of a time you suffered as a normal part of life and then saw God bring great good out of your sufferings?
5. What Scriptures come to mind when you think of Sabina and her life?
6. Can you share about a time when you suffered for being a Christian? How did you handle it? Did God help you? What was the outcome?

TWO

Elisabeth Elliot:
The Gift of Widowhood

Elisabeth Elliot, a young mother and a widow, clutched her two-year-old daughter's hand as they trudged through the steamy jungles of Ecuador, South America. With another missionary, they were following a native Indian through the jungles to a camp of the tribe who had murdered her husband. As the jungle vines snapped on her face, she lifted up her daughter to carry her and shield her from the jungle growth. Surely she had doubts and misgivings. Would they accept her? Would she be able to love and forgive them from her heart? How would her daughter fare living with such a savage tribe? Elisabeth was determined to love them, to win them to Christ, and to spread the gospel.

Called Betty by close friends, Elisabeth was first famous for her book *Through Gates of Splendor*, in which she chronicled the death of her now famous missionary husband, Jim Elliot. Born on October 8, 1927, Jim Elliot was an evangelical Christian. He was speared to death on January 8, 1956, while attempting to make contact with the Auca Indians in Ecuador, South America. Also called the Huaorani tribe, the Aucas were known as savages by their neighbors. Auca means "savage" in the language of the Quechuas, who lived nearby.

Jim Elliot believed he was called to missions and that God was calling him to work in Ecuador, spreading the gospel among the heathen tribes. He is famous for a quote in one of his journals as he contemplated the possible outcomes of working with unreached people groups. "He is no fool who gives what he cannot keep to gain that which he cannot lose," he wrote. We apply this truth in hindsight to the loss of his life at such a young age. It could be that God was preparing him to give his life for the gospel of Jesus Christ.

Jim Elliot and Elisabeth (her maiden name was Howard) had admitted to each other that they were attracted to and interested in each other, but Jim felt strongly that he would be most effective as a single missionary. For five years they prayed for each other, corresponded, saw each other on rare occasions, and remained celibate. But as Jim's good friends who were headed for the mission field married, Jim decided to marry. He married Elisabeth on October 8, 1953. They were married in Ecuador in Quito, a headquarters for missionaries. She told me it was definitely worth the wait.

Elisabeth stayed behind with the other wives, praying as their husbands approached the Aucas. Elisabeth, with the wives of Ed McCully, Roger Youderian, Pete Fleming, and Nate Saint, their pilot, were praying for the safety and the success of their husbands. The five missionaries camped upstream from the Aucas and made contact with one Auca Indian, who they thought was convinced of their good intentions. But evidently this tribesman went back and told his comrades that the missionaries were ill intentioned. The Auca Indians then decided the five men must die. As the missionaries walked upstream to make contact, several warriors from the Auca tribe met them and speared all five to death. Their wives were stunned and heartbroken when they heard of their husbands' fate.

Elisabeth was a strong and disciplined person who had a courageous faith in her Savior, Jesus Christ. She was completely at one with her husband's intentions to reach the Aucas with the gospel. After his death, she continued the missionary work and ultimately went to live with the Aucas, taking with her their two-year-old daughter, Valerie.

(After several years, she married a seminary professor who later died of cancer. Her third and last husband, Lars Gren, when I interviewed him, told me that she had no fear when she took her young daughter to live with the Aucas. He said that her faith in God was so strong that there was no room for fear.)

While she was working with the Quechua Indians, Elisabeth was taught the language of the Aucas by several Indian women. This prepared her to respond when an opening came to go work and live with the Huaoranis. In 1958, she and Valerie went with fellow missionary Rachel Saint to live with the tribe of Indians that had killed her husband. The Auca/Huaorani tribe gave her the nickname Gikari, which means "woodpecker" in their language. Many of the tribe became Christians and began evangelizing neighboring tribes. Elisabeth has long been admired for her bravery in going to live with such a hostile tribe, taking their daughter to show God's love to those who had murdered her husband. Anyone who knew Elisabeth Elliott knew her to be fearless with a boundless trust in her heavenly Father.

She returned to work with the Quechua Indians until 1963 when she moved back to the United States with Valerie, who was then thirteen.

In 1969, Elisabeth married Addison Leitch, a professor of theology at Gordon-Conwell Theological Seminary in South Hamilton, Massachusetts.

He died of cancer in 1973. Elisabeth became an adjunct professor at Gordon-Conwell, where she taught her popular course Christian Expression. In one of my visits with her, she told me that this course was basically about manners and that some Christian young people badly needed that kind of instruction.

In 1977, Elisabeth Elliot Leitch married Lars Gren, a hospital chaplain. Theirs was a very happy and compatible match. They worked, traveled, and wrote together. During the 1970s she had worked as a stylistic consultant for the committee translating the New International Version of the Bible. She is listed as one of its contributors. In 1981, she was appointed writer-in-residence at Gordon College in Wenham, Massachusetts.

From 1988 to 2001 Elisabeth could be heard daily on her radio program, *Gateway to Joy*, produced by the Good News Broadcasting Association of Lincoln, Nebraska. She kept her name as Elisabeth Elliot. She usually opened the program by saying, "You are loved with an everlasting love—that's what the Bible says—and underneath are the everlasting arms. This is your friend Elisabeth Elliot." Her broadcasts continued on many stations long after her entrance into glory. She urged her listeners never to waste their pain and to always enjoy and make the most of whatever season they found themselves in. She taught that life is a gift, and that even widowhood and loneliness are gifts if used in the service of the Lord.

In her later years, Elisabeth and Lars kept in touch with the body of Christ through mail and through their website. She died in Magnolia, Massachusetts, on June 15, 2015, at the age of eighty-eight. She was deeply mourned and is greatly missed.

During her lifetime, she was well known as a speaker and an author. Besides publishing *Through Gates of Splendor* and *The Journals of Jim Elliot*, she wrote many other books. One of my favorites is *A Slow and Certain Light*, in which she said she wrote "everything I personally know about God's guidance."[4] It is a wonderful book, and I highly recommend it.

She compares our adventure of life with a trip down the jungles of the Amazon. She said if you plan to travel through the jungle, you do not need a book on all the things that might happen to you and what you need to do to prepare. She says what you need is a person, a personal guide. This is what Jesus is to us. The Bible gives us many principles, much information, and much wisdom, but there is no substitute for walking closely with Jesus Himself and having Him as our personal guide through the treacherous paths of life.

[4] Elisabeth Elliot, *A Slow and Certain Light: God's Guidance*, 2nd ed., (Fleming H. Revell, 1997).

Another of her books that touched me deeply was *Passion and Purity.* When they were in college, Jim told her that he loved her but that he believed he would be more effective as a single missionary than a married one. Elisabeth accepted this and prayed a lot about her struggles with being a single woman. For Elisabeth and her Christian friends, single Christian life meant no sex before marriage. They were convinced that this was what the Scriptures taught and what God had revealed as His perfect will.

Elisabeth had to wait for five years from the time Jim Elliot told her that he loved her until the time they were married. They were both outstanding people and are excellent examples for those of us living in our confused and immoral culture.

In her book *Passion and Purity*, Elisabeth confessed what a difficult time they'd had waiting and not becoming physically intimate. They were extremely attracted to each other, but both believed that God was counseling them to wait. Jim was sincere in his desire to serve God, and he had been advised by other missionaries that he would be more effective for the Lord if he were single. So they waited.

Elisabeth spent much time in prayer and in Scripture and sought God's help in having to wait for Jim. They both agreed that it was worth the wait. But it was a battle.

She explains the battle in *Passion and Purity*.[5] "The confusion that followed my earnest prayers is not surprising to me now. If there is an enemy of souls (and I have not the slightest doubt that there is), one thing he cannot abide is our desire for purity. Hence a man or woman's passions become a major battleground. The Lover of our Souls does not prevent this. I was perplexed because it seemed to me He should prevent it, but He doesn't. He wants us to learn to use our weapons." She described women she had counseled who longed to be married, had fallen in love too quickly, and ended up confused. It seems there is always that yearning for marriage.

She found the agonizing prayers and waiting difficult to endure, but Elisabeth believed that the process was purifying her heart. She believed that the decision to stay chaste until marriage was purging the sin out of her heart. It was a lot of hard work, she related, to bring her unruly affections into proper order. She and Jim both poured their energies into seeking and serving God and preparing for missionary work. Elisabeth told me she took very seriously a quotation from the *Book of Common Prayer* for the fifth Sunday after Lent:

> Almighty God, you alone can bring into order
> the unruly wills and affections of sinners. Grant

---

[5] Elisabeth Elliot, *Passion and Purity* (Old Tappan, New Jersey: Power Books: Fleming H. Revell Company, 1984), 26.

your people grace to love what you command
and desire what you promise; that, among the
swift and varied changes of the world, our hearts
may surely there be fixed where true joys are to
be found; through Jesus Christ our Lord, who
lives and reigns with you and the Holy Spirit,
one God, now and forever, Amen.[6]

Jim Elliot felt called to serve God in Ecuador,
and I do not blame Elisabeth for going to Ecuador
herself to prepare for mission work. I am sure she
felt led by God to do so, and God may have sent
her there preparing her to be a future wife for Jim.

Another one of her books that I have loved is
Discipline, the Glad Surrender. In it one can see
what an intellectual and a deep thinker she was,
as well as a practical and devoted disciple of Jesus.

The closer one comes to the center of things,
the better able he is to observe the connections.
Everything created is connected, for everything
is produced by the same mind, the same love,
and is dependent on the same Creator. He who
masterminded the universe, the Lord God Om-
nipotent, is the One who called the stars into
being, commanded light, spoke the Word that
brought about the existence of time and space

---

[6] The Book of Common Prayer was first introduced in England in 1549. Later editions can still be found on Amazon.
This link will take you to the prayer Elisabeth cited: https://
en.wikisource.org/wiki/Page:Book_of_common_prayer_
(TEC,_1979).pdf/255.

and every form of matter: salt and stone, rose and redwood, feather and fur and fin and flesh.[7]

In this excellent book, Elisabeth discussed the ramifications of discipline on discipleship in many areas. She touched on body, mind, and spirit as well as time, possessions, work, and feelings. I don't believe I have ever been challenged as much to be completely devoted to Jesus as I was in this book.

Getting Personal

Elisabeth's dramatic actions, showing love and forgiveness toward those who murdered her husband, set an example for me. We all have to forgive many people for many issues. It is a blessing to obey in earnest Jesus's commands in Luke 6 to love, pray for, bless, and do good to your enemies.

> But to you who are listening I say: Love your enemies, do good to those who hate you, bless those who cruse you, pray for those who mistreat you. If someone slaps you on one cheek, turn to them the other also. If someone takes your coat, do not withhold your shirt from them. Give to everyone who asks you, and if anyone takes what belongs to you, do not demand it back. (Luke 6:27–30 NIV).

---

[7] Elisabeth Elliot, *Discipline, the Glad Surrender* (Grand Rapids, Michigan: Revell, 1982), 10.

Praying for those who hurt me helped me avoid the negative results Jesus warns about in the eighteenth chapter of Matthew. In that parable, a servant was forgiven a huge amount by his master, and then he refused to forgive even a small amount owed by a fellow servant. "In anger his master turned him over to the jailers until he should pay back all he owed. This is how my heavenly Father will treat each of you unless you forgive your brother from your heart" (Matt. 18:34–35).

Praying for those who had hurt me was probably the single most effective practice I did when forgiving others. I had learned in Al-Anon and in the *Big Book of Alcoholics Anonymous* that to forgive someone, you should pray for that person for everything you want for yourself, daily for two weeks. I tried this and it worked beautifully. It healed me of my anger and actually turned my heart from hatred and bitterness to love and forgiveness. Since I wanted a great deal for myself, it was easy to pray for a long time for my enemies.

On one occasion, I had dinner with Elisabeth Elliot in the French Quarter in New Orleans, with my good friend Chaplain Hy McEnery. I was newly married and trying to be organized, disciplined, productive, and loving. Elisabeth was tall, athletic, tanned, and confident. I knew her story, so I was thrilled to meet her in person. It was an honor to talk with and listen to her. I so wanted to be disciplined, productive, brave, and strong. Elisabeth shone in those character traits. I was thrilled to meet her and must confess I idolized her.

I was fortunate to hear Elisabeth speak to the wives of seminary students at Dallas Theological Seminary in 1979. She impressed me as being very serious, deep, and thoughtful. I still have my notes from her talk, during which she said our main goal should be to know God. She stressed that obedience is the first step toward that goal. Using Noah as an example, she said that the evidence of faith is obedience. She pointed out that when Abraham obeyed, his feelings were not recorded in the Bible.

It is more important to obey God, no matter how we feel, than it is to act out our feelings. Elisabeth comforted us with the perspective that our circumstances are a gift. If we are in the middle of difficult circumstances, these can be transformed and can become a blessing if we come to know Jesus Christ. It is simple, but not easy. We must trust and obey.

She told us wives of Dallas Theological Seminary that one time she was reading from 1 Peter 4:12–13: "Dear friends, do not be surprised at the painful trial you are suffering, as though something strange were happening to you. But rejoice that you participate in the sufferings of Christ, so that you may be overjoyed when His glory is revealed."

Shortly after reading that, she said, she found that a whole year's work translating the Bible into the native language had been accidentally burned up. She never discovered the purpose of that suffering, and she started over and redid all the work.

During her speech to us at Dallas Seminary, she declared, "Nothing can happen to you or to anyone you love for which God has not *already made provision!*"

I was thrilled to hear a Christian woman who believed this, who had been through as many painful events as Elisabeth Elliot! This has been a principle that has helped me in many situations through the years. I now agree with Elisabeth that this is true. If God is all good, all powerful, and all wise, and loves us totally and unconditionally, then this maxim is not beyond a dedicated Christian's belief.

Elisabeth Elliot's courage and love in living with the savage tribe whose members had speared her husband to death still takes my breath away. Was she not afraid? I am sure she had direction from God to make the move, but wasn't she still human? Having met her I believe she would have said, "No, I was not afraid. I knew that God would protect us and that this is what He was asking me to do." But in my heart of hearts, I still marvel at her tenacity and strength. Sometimes when I am afraid, driving in the dark of night, or acting as an attorney going before a new judge with a harsh reputation for a hearing, I think of Elisabeth Elliot and I find new courage.

I met Elisabeth's daughter, Valerie, after she was grown and married. Once when my then-husband and I were at a house party with the McIlhennys on Avery Island, Valerie's husband was preaching at the small local church, and we all went to hear him. She and her husband came to the McIlhennys' for lunch. My husband and I had had a fight and were not speaking to each other. I asked Valerie for advice. She said we should both get down on our knees and confess our sins out loud to each other. We did, and the problem disappeared immediately.

Let's Talk

1. What impresses you most about Elisabeth Elliot's life and character?
2. What do you think of her husband, Jim Elliot's, life?
3. What Scriptures come to mind when you think of Jim and Elisabeth and their lives?
4. How would you feel if your spouse was killed on the mission field? Would you be angry with God? What would you tell your children? Would you go to live with and minister to the people who killed him?
5. Do you think Elisabeth's commitment to moral purity is outdated or old-fashioned? What do you believe Scripture says about intimacy before marriage?
6. Have you ever gone on a mission trip or thought you might be called to missions?

Three

Susanna Wesley: Magnificent Motherhood

The parsonage was on fire, and Susanna's five-year-old son was calling down from an upper window surrounded by flames. It was too far to jump safely, and he was terrified at the prospect of jumping out of a window from the second story. A kind neighbor stood on another man's shoulders and gently lifted the young boy out of the fire and down to the ground and safety. Shortly after the young John Wesley was rescued, the burning roof crashed into the room where he had been standing. This episode convinced Susanna that God had spared John's life for a special purpose.[8]

Susanna Wesley was the amazing mother of John Wesley, who was an evangelist, a revivalist, and the founder of the Methodist church.

The life of Susanna Wesley is a powerful an-

---

[8] Arnold A. Dallimore, *Susannah Wesley* (Grand Rapids, Michigan: Baker Book House, 1994), 6.

tidote for any woman today who is having a hard time raising her family. There is a traditional story about her that may or not be true. Legend has it that she would sit on the floor in the middle of her kitchen and throw her apron over her head. This was a sign to her children that she should then be left alone to pray. If that story is true, then her prayer life was a top priority.

Her husband, Samuel Wesley, favored their sons over their daughters. One of their daughters was married off to an uneducated, boorish man who treated her badly. Samuel spent most of what little money they had on unprofitable pursuits and left Susanna for long periods of time in dire circumstances.

Susanna was born in England in 1669 during a time when Christianity was in turmoil. To appreciate Susanna and the tremendous achievements of her sons John and Charles Wesley, we need an understanding of the development of Christianity in England.

In 597 AD, Pope Gregory the First sent Saint Augustine of Canterbury (not Monica's son) to evangelize the people of Britain. After this, the Church of England remained under the authority of the Roman Catholic Church for centuries. Sharp divisions erupted in 1517 when Martin Luther posted his *Ninety-five Theses* and started the Protestant Reformation. The Church of England formally separated from the Church of Rome in 1534 under King Henry VIII for political reasons and to allow him to divorce and remarry. This separation started more than a century of painful struggle between various religious factions.

In 1620, the persecuted Christians left England to worship in America. They sought freedom to worship God according to their consciences. From 1649 to 1660, the Puritans dominated England, headed by Oliver Cromwell. They wanted to purify the church. Susanna Wesley's father, Samuel Annesley, was an ordained minister, educated, well-off, and a respected Christian leader. He was sympathetic to the Puritans and published a collection of sermons by some of the most prestigious ministers in England.

In 1662, seven years before Susanna was born, the Church of England proclaimed itself the one and only true religion. The Act of Uniformity decreed that all Church of England ministers must use the accepted form of the Book of Common Prayer or be forced out of their parishes. The formal liturgy and the lack of godliness of many Church of England priests distressed serious Protestants. About two thousand ministers refused to conform and were banned from Anglican pulpits. Those excluded were called "Non-conformists" or "Dissenters." Susanna's father, Samuel Annesley, was one of the leading Non-conformists. His spacious and comfortable home became a center for Christians who believed that the Church of England needed serious reform.

Susanna was the youngest of Samuel Annesley's twenty-five children. She was serious about Christianity at an early age. An earnest student, she learned Greek and Hebrew and studied the Scriptures. Susanna was educated at home and learned to think for herself. She developed a confidence in her own judgment, which was remarkable for a woman in the sixteen hundreds. Many well-educated visitors enjoyed the intellectual and spiritual stimulation of the Annesley home and broadened Susanna's horizons. After her father became a leading Non-conformist, he suffered financially but was still able to provide for his family.

At the age of thirteen, Susanna decided upon purely theological grounds to leave the Non-conformist party and join the established Church of England.[9] After Oliver Cromwell's Protectorate ended in 1660, King Charles II restored the Church of England to a moderate form of worship, emphasizing the Reformation doctrine of justification by faith. The traditional doctrinal positions of orthodox Christianity were set forth in the *Thirty-Nine Articles*. Susanna held them in high esteem and passed on this mindset to her children. Her most famous son, John Wesley, adapted them

[9] C. E. Vulliamy, *John Wesley* (Westwood, New Jersey: Barbour and Company Inc., 1985), 2.

for the American Methodists when he founded a church in Savannah, Georgia.

Susanna was a beautiful woman with many accomplishments.[10] She had high standards and a cheerful disposition. She is thought to have met her husband, Samuel Wesley, at her father's home in London. Samuel Wesley, the son of another Non-conformist minister, was a serious student. Like Susanna, he had decided to align himself with the established Church of England.

They were married and had high hopes for a good position in the Anglican Church. Unfortunately, Samuel Wesley's connections failed to produce advantageous appointments. The young couple found themselves assigned to serve the ignorant and barbaric peasants of Epworth, a poor village in Lincolnshire. The Wesleys were treated cruelly by the villagers. Some of the people of Epworth resented the couple, and history does not tell us why. Perhaps it was because Samuel was a stern High Churchman and a vocal critic of the Non-conformists. Maybe it was just the brutal and vicious nature of the inhabitants. Whatever the reason, they threatened him, rioted outside of the rectory, stabbed his cows, and in 1702 tried to burn down the Epworth Rectory by throwing fire upon the thatched roof.[11]

Hardship and deprivation were the constant

[10] Vulliamy, *John Wesley*, 2.

[11] Vulliamy, *John Wesley*, 4.

companions of Susanna Wesley as she struggled to raise her children. She gave birth nineteen times, but only nine of her children survived infancy.

One historian stated that Susanna's husband suffered from poor political judgment and a total incapacity for the management of his own affairs. Although he received a modest salary from the Church of England as rector of the village of Epworth in Lincolnshire, the family was very poor. Samuel Wesley was once imprisoned for his debts. Susanna's father did not help them and left her nothing in his will, perhaps because of their repudiation of the Non-conformist movement.

Although Susanna must have felt keenly the hardships of poverty, she was not a complainer. Records of her family evidence a strong and courageous woman who believed God had called her to bring up her children in the nurture and admonition of the Lord as directed in Ephesians 6:4. She devoted herself to their education. She was determined to teach them manners, Christian character, and correct doctrine. As a woman, Susanna Wesley was barred from the educational institutions of her day. Many intelligent Puritan women in the seventeenth century focused their energies on their homes. To them it was a ministry from God to raise their children to be devout Christians.

Susanna was very disciplined and educated her children by herself at home. Her husband was accustomed to long absences as he pursued his interests in London. Family letters do not show her husband to have been involved in their children's education. Susanna set up methods of teaching with strict schedules. When a child was five years old, she began his or her systematic education. She taught school from nine in the morning until twelve noon and from two to five in the afternoon. She used methods of patient repetition and was amazed at how much a young child could learn through consistent application. By today's standards, she may seem a little too strict, legalistic, and rigid. "The first thing to be done with children," declared Mrs. Wesley "is to conquer their will." In her circumstances, it was an effective way to produce disciplined and competent offspring.

Susanna's son John Wesley, founder of Methodism, was her fifteenth child. His older brother Samuel was a faithful but stern minister who did not approve of John's informal methods of evangelism. John's more amiable brother Charles was a devoted lifelong friend and ally who worked with him to evangelize the working classes of Great Britain.

The need for evangelism in the lower classes of England in the seventeen hundreds cannot be over-emphasized. Uneducated peasants and farmers were heartless and barbaric in their treatment of their enemies. The established Church of England appealed to the nobility and the upper classes. According to historians, the working classes were largely ignored and were expected to be cruel and brutal. The landowners and upper classes feared that if the working classes were educated or evangelized, either they would not work or they would demand higher wages.

When John and Charles worked to bring true Christianity to laborers and farmers, they faced mobs and violence. Their lives were threatened. God always delivered them, but it was not easy. Growing up in difficult circumstances with a godly, disciplined mother prepared John and Charles Wesley for ministry. They were prepared to start and sustain one of the greatest Christian revivals in history.

Coming from a comfortable and privileged background, living in the harsh deprivations of a poor village, often without the support or companionship of her husband, Susanna suffered greatly. But from her sufferings emerged a family that produced two of the greatest Christian lights of the seventeenth century. Her devotion to God and her endurance while suffering reminds me of the passage in 1 Peter: "For this finds favor, if for the sake of conscience toward God a man bears up under sorrows when suffering unjustly. For what credit is there if, when you sin and are harshly treated, you endure it with patience? But if when you do what is right and suffer for it you patiently endure it, this finds favor with God. For you have been called for this purpose, since Christ also suffered for you, leaving you an example for you to follow in His steps" (1 Peter 2:19–21 NASB).

When her husband died, Susanna was left impoverished and looked to the charity of her children to survive. As a new widow living with one of her daughters, she wrote to her son John, expressing her devotion to God:

> I have long since chosen Him for my only good, my all; my pleasure, my happiness in this world as in the world to come. . . . Yet I do not long to go home, as in reason I ought to do. This often shocks me; and as I constantly pray (almost without ceasing) for thee, my son, so I beg you likewise to pray for me, that God would make me better, and take me at the best.
> Your loving mother,
> Susanna Wesley[12]

Getting Personal

Reading about and contemplating the life of Susanna Wesley was for me a sure cure for self-pity. I have fought self-pity often in my life, and remembering Susanna helps me to be more thankful for all that the Lord has given me.

After my divorce, there were times when I was so lonely I didn't think I could stand it. I normally feel the Lord's presence, but I remember one time

---

[12] Dallimore, *Susannah Wesley*, 157.

being so lonely that I couldn't feel God's presence at all. I knew intellectually that He was with me, but the loneliness was so dramatic that I felt very much alone. Remembering Susanna's suffering helped me to endure and get through hard times. God truly is always with us.

Comparing my life to hers motivates me to thank and praise God for being so kind and gracious to me. When I was married, we struggled to make ends meet, but we never lacked for food, clothing, or housing. Often when I was working in my kitchen when the children were young, I would think of Susanna sitting in the middle of her kitchen floor with her apron over her head, praying. The children knew when she covered her head with her apron that they were not to interrupt her as she was praying. If she could face and overcome all of her difficulties, then I could face and overcome my own challenges.

In my family of origin, I was blessed to have grown up in a comfortable home where we lacked for nothing important. I cannot imagine how Susanna lived and accomplished as much as she did. She worked hard, grew vegetables, milked cows, cooked meals, homeschooled the children, and fulfilled the duties of a minister's wife. How she did all of this is beyond my imagination. She taught her children by example to work hard as well as to read the Bible and pray.

Let's Talk

1. What do you think about the events that caused Susanna so much suffering?
2. What do you think of her having given birth nineteen times?
3. What do you think of her homeschooling her children? Were you surprised to learn that people homeschooled that long ago?
4. What Scriptures come to mind when you consider Susanna Wesley's life?
5. What do you know about the Methodist church, then and now?
6. What do you know about the great revivals of the seventeen hundreds?
7. How much do you think Susanna influenced John Wesley?

Four

Monica: The Woman Who Never Gave Up

Monica pulled on her son's clothing, crying pitifully. "Please, please, let me go with you," she begged. Her son was about to sail to another town in Italy, and she desperately wanted to go with him.

"No, Mother," he answered. "You cry too much, and you would be a great burden to me. Go home and take care of your other children. I am dedicated to my career, and you would only hurt my chances of success."

Such a scene might well have occurred as Monica prayed for her son and followed him all over Italy for almost eighteen years.

Saint Augustine's mother's name was Monica, and she is known as Saint Monica by the Catholic church. She was a passionate woman who loved and trusted God. She raised her children in the

Christian faith, was long suffering with her husband, and faithful in Christian service. She prayed for her son for eighteen years, following him from city to city in Italy while he rejected her and her Christian faith.

Monica was born in 331 AD in Tagaste, Numidia, in what is now the eastern part of Algeria in North Africa.[13] She was raised by devout Christian parents. She had an arranged marriage to an older government official named Patricius. He had a good position but did not share her faith and was ill tempered.

One thing we know for certain is that Monica suffered greatly in her marriage. Any Christian woman married to a man who rejects her faith in God knows how difficult this is. Monica prayed that God would touch her husband's heart and convert him to Christianity. Historians believe that Patricius had an uncontrollable temper, a powerful sex drive, and was capable of being brutal and verbally abusive. History records how beautifully and patiently Monica suffered until God answered her prayers for her husband, who came to a saving faith in Jesus Christ before he died. She didn't just "suffer" but raised three children and lived a life of prayer and service.

It is recorded in Augustine's *Confessions*[14] and

[13] Giovanni Falbo, *Saint Monica, The Power of a Mother's Love* (Boston: Pauline Books and Media, 2007), 1.

[14] Augustine, *Confessions*, trans. F. J. Sheed (New York: Sheed and Ward, 1943), 197.

accepted by historians[15] that Patricius was guilty of committing adultery. The legendary tears Monica shed praying for her son may have had other sources. The fact that God answered Monica's prayers for her son is a great encouragement to modern women. But in regard to Monica's suffering, Augustine recorded that in relation to her husband, she bore his acts of unfaithfulness quietly.[16]

Monica was not only passionate and prayerful but also practical. She understood that the fourth century marriage contract gave a married woman almost no rights or recourse to protect her from abuse. Monica worked around her husband, being patient and quiet until his temper cooled. She counseled other married women that they were essentially servants and that to stand up to abuse was to invite further mistreatment. Augustine explains in his *Confessions* that his mother knew that a wife must not resist an angry husband. His mother would wait patiently until Patricius was calm and quiet again, and then she would explain her actions.[17]

One of the greatest heartbreaks for a Christian woman married to a man who does not follow Jesus is the detrimental effect this situation can have on their children. Although Patricius died when Augustine was seventeen, Patricius had come to a

---

[15] Falbo, 18.

[16] Augustine, *Confessions*, 197.

[17] Augustine, *Confessions*, 197.

saving faith before dying. Augustine followed in his father's earlier footsteps when it came to women. Patricius bragged to Monica about what he called Augustine's "ripening manhood" and did little to curb his son's sensual appetites. Failing to teach chastity, morality, and faithfulness in marriage, he encouraged promiscuity and fornication. Augustine followed his father's example of waywardness.[18] He lived with a woman without marrying her and they had a son. The son later became a Christian, but the situation was complicated. Augustine describes his tortuous spiritual journey back to God in his *Confessions* and confides that one of the main factors delaying his total surrender was his carnal need for a woman.[19]

Augustine, Monica's firstborn son, was born in 354 AD in Tagaste. Monica raised him, his brother, Navigius, and his sister, Perpetua, in the nurture and admonition of the Lord as prescribed in Ephesians 6:4. Navigius never caused her any difficulty. Perpetua embraced Christianity and became the head of a monastery for women after she was widowed.[20] Augustine listened seriously to Monica's teachings when he was young, but as a teenager he turned away from God.

At age eleven in 365 AD, Augustine was sent to

---

[18] Falbo, 18.

[19] Augustine, *Confessions*, 58.

[20] Pope Benedict XVI, *Church Fathers from Clement of Rome to Augustine* (San Francisco: Ignatius Press, 2008), 169.

a boarding school in Madaurus, a small Numidian city eighteen miles south of Tagaste in what is present day Algeria. There he did extremely well in his studies of Latin and grammar but was also taught pagan beliefs and practices. He excelled in rhetoric and was thought by his parents to have bright prospects for success in a political life. He tells us in his *Confessions* that he planned to become a lawyer and was determined to shine. He confesses that he believed that the less honest he was, the more famous he would be.

Augustine's parents greatly valued education.[21] His father was not rich but worked hard to raise the funds necessary for Augustine's schooling. Augustine told his parents after his conversion that his classical education was woefully lacking in moral character. In his *Confessions,* he goes into great detail about the dangers to a young mind inherent in the studies he was forced to take. His warnings laid a foundation for Christian education for future generations.

Augustine was forced to study the gods of Olympus as embellished by Homer, who were adulterers and thieves and, according to Augustine, prepared men to be equally immoral with no scruples. He warned that this study was detrimental to the development of good character.[22]

---

[21] Pope Benedict XVI, *Church Fathers from Clement of Rome to Augustine*, 29.

[22] Pope Benedict XVI, *Church Fathers from Clement of Rome to Augustine*, 19.

Furthering his pagan education, Augustine was sent to study in Carthage, a prominent city in Tunisia in North Africa. Extremely intelligent and sensitive, he was consciously seeking truth and answers to life's questions in philosophy and classical literature. By the time he was seventeen, he had been greatly influenced by Gnosticism[23] and Neoplatonism. In Carthage, he became a follower of theories that the Christian church believed to be heretical. He was studying there in 371 AD when his father died.

As Augustine turned his back on Christianity, he totally rejected his mother. The knowledge that Jesus was a man of sorrows, despised and rejected and acquainted with grief, may have comforted Monica, but the emotional pain of rejection runs deep. The wounds and hurts from the rejection of her son may have been one of the reasons she was known as a woman who cried daily. After her husband died, Monica devoted her prayers and heart's desires to her son.

Augustine refers to his mother's tears and her prayers many times in his *Confessions,* but he thinks she cried too much. Before his conversion, he was not sympathetic to her concerns for his soul. She was so intent on his conversion that she followed him from city to city.

After teaching rhetoric and grammar in Car-

---

[23] Gnosticism—a dualistic philosophy thought to be heresy by the Roman Catholic Church.

thage for nine years, he was becoming disillusioned with the heretical philosophies he had been enamored of. He was offered a teaching position in Rome and decided to leave Carthage and sail to Rome.

Monica followed him to the seacoast and begged him to come home with her or take her to Rome with him. He confesses that he lied to his mother, tricked her into staying in a place near the ship, and sailed at night without telling her. He felt she was too attached to him. He later noted that while she was praying to prevent his passage to Rome, God knew that the move would ultimately answer her greatest prayer, which was that Augustine would return to God with all of his heart.

His devotion to several popular heresies so upset his mother that on one occasion she could not eat at the same table with him. Then God spoke to her in a dream and told her that one day Augustine would stand with her on truth. She believed the vision and knew that Augustine would one day return to God and Christianity. Augustine himself was deeply moved by this communication to his mother from God.

After he returned to God, he describes his mother as a chaste, God-fearing, and sober widow[24] and wrote that the vision God had given her cheered her up and kept her hopeful during the dif-

---

[24] Augustine, *Confessions*.

ficult years of waiting for his conversion. Augustine confided in his *Confessions* that he realized God had been speaking to him through his mother when she warned him not to sin with women, above all not with any man's wife.

He says he knew that God was speaking to him through his mother, and that in ignoring her he was ignoring God. Augustine ultimately became a godly, celibate man of God and described Monica as a woman in sex, with the faith of a man, with the serenity of great age, the love of a mother, the piety of a Christian.

After a time in Rome, Augustine was offered a professorship of rhetoric and moved to Milan. Monica followed him to Rome, found that he had moved to Milan, and followed him there. On the sea journey from her home in Africa to Italy, she reassured the sailors in a storm that God would keep them safe because He had given her promises through visions of the salvation of her son.

St. Ambrose, the Bishop of Milan at that time, was preaching Christ effectively. Monica went to him and begged him to help win her son back to Christianity. St. Ambrose was sympathetic but counseled her that talking to him at this point would prove fruitless. Yet it was Augustine's exposure to Ambrose's preaching Sunday after Sunday that ultimately brought him back to faith in Jesus Christ.

St. Ambrose had been appointed Bishop of Milan in 374 AD by popular acclaim. Although he felt completely unqualified for the position, he began studying ardently. He was a gifted speaker and gave Augustine a new understanding of the depths and truths of Scripture. After Augustine was converted, he continued to be influenced by St. Ambrose's preaching.

Augustine tells in great detail in his *Confessions* of his struggles with philosophy and his tortuous search for truth before his dramatic conversion.[25] He sensed that God was calling him, but turning from his philosophies and his hedonistic lifestyle caused great agonies of soul. He was struggling to repent. He says he was sick at heart and in torment, accusing himself with a new intensity of bitterness, twisting and turning in his chain in the hope that it might be utterly broken.[26] In a garden, he flung himself under a fig tree and cried bitter tears. He asked God how long he was going to have to suffer before he received the grace to surrender.

Suddenly he says he heard a child's voice from a nearby house singing, "Take and read, take and read." He took this as a divine command to open the Scriptures and read and heed whatever passage he opened to. Augustine's return to Christ came on August 15, 386 AD.[27] He opened to Paul's Epistle

[25] Augustine, *Confessions*, 176.

[26] Augustine, *Confessions*, 175.

[27] Pope Benedict XVI, *Church Fathers from Clement of Rome to Augustine*, 171.

to the Romans, chapter 13, verses 13–14: "Let us behave properly as in the day, not in carousing and drunkenness, not in sexual promiscuity and sensuality, not in strife and jealousy. But put on the Lord Jesus Christ, and make no provision for the flesh in regard to its lusts" (NASB).

He rushed inside to tell his mother, who was overjoyed at the prayed-for and longed-for news. She praised God for answering her prayers and remembering her tears. Augustine felt a light and confidence flood his soul that washed away the darkness and uncertainty. He wrote that he no longer wanted a wife or a woman or any of the world's temptations, but stood by his mother in faith, fulfilling the vision God had given her.[28] Monica is an example of the truth of the Scripture, "Those who sow in tears shall reap with joyful shouting" (Ps. 126:5 NASB).

Monica was devout. She gave alms to the poor, as was the custom of pious Christians in the fourth century. While in North Africa, she practiced the tradition of bringing food, bread, and wine for the poor to private prayer chapels built in memory of the saints. When St. Ambrose, Bishop of Milan, forbade the practice for fear of encouraging gluttony and drunkenness, she complied. She also gave up her habit of fasting on Saturdays. In Milan, Christians ate on Saturdays. Ambrose counseled

---

[28] Augustine, *Confessions*, 179.

her that when in Rome, he would eat and do as the Romans do, and in Milan he would do otherwise. This is where we get the saying "When in Rome, do as the Romans do."

In his *Confessions,* Augustine credits his return to the Christian faith to the prayers of his mother. Augustine's great love and passion for God and his burning desire to know Him and serve Him are evident. He asks God to grant him the grace to know his Lord. He calls God his glory and his life, the God of his heart. He prays in his *Confessions*, "O Thou, the Power of my soul," and "my inmost Physician."[29] He calls Him "My Father, My Protector," "my true Life, my God," and "O truly good and certain Loveliness."[30] He calls out, "You, God, who are Truth, my Light, the salvation of my countenance and my God."[31]

Augustine's desire to know God, to love and understand Him, permeates his whole *Confessions*. "Great art Thou, O Lord, and greatly to be praised; great is Thy power, and of Thy wisdom there is no number. And man desires to praise Thee . . . For Thou hast made us for Thyself, and our hearts are restless till they rest in Thee."[32]

The summation of Augustine's life and contributions shows the breadth of God's answers to

---

[29] Augustine, *Confessions*, 211.

[30] Augustine, *Confessions*, 228.

[31] Augustine, *Confessions*, 233.

[32] Augustine, *Confessions*, 8.

Monica's prayers. Augustine's writings were profoundly influential in the development of Christianity and Western philosophy and culture. Many consider him the father of the Latin church.[33] He wrote and numbered over a thousand writings that were copied, studied, and widely read.

Augustine reveled in his renewed relationship with his God, with his beloved Lord Jesus Christ. He experienced a deep and personal relationship with God. He writes, "I talked with You as friends talk, my glory and my riches and my salvation, my Lord God."[34]

Monica's life is an example of a fulfilled promise of James 5:16, "The effective prayer of a righteous man can accomplish much" (NASB). Fervent and persevering, Monica was a woman of great faith. Scripture tells us that "Without faith it is impossible to please Him, for he who comes to God must believe that He is, and that He is a rewarder of those who seek Him" (Heb. 11:6 NASB). Monica was a woman greatly pleasing to God and a great encouragement to me.

Getting Personal

There is probably no more painful path we can experience than that resulting from rejection. It is

[33] Pope Benedict XVI, *Church Fathers from Clement of Rome to Augustine*, 167.

[34] Pope Benedict XVI, *Church Fathers from Clement of Rome to Augustine*, 183.

like death in a way because you lose the relationship completely.

When some relatives rejected me, I thought the emotional pain was going to make me ill. In fact, it did, as the stress from strained relationships with these families caused me great intestinal distress.

I called my counselor and had a great session facing my part in the breakup. When I had examined my heart and repented of my own attitudes of judgment, taking offense, of taking things personally, I started once again the delicate process of forgiveness.

I say it is a delicate process because it is so easy to believe we have forgiven someone when we still harbor bitterness, resentment, or unforgiveness in our hearts. It is a matter of deep prayer and working with the Holy Spirit to discover if we truly have forgiven. Only Jesus can assure us that we have truly forgiven. If we have a true heart of love for the one who has hurt us, as He has commanded us in the sixth chapter of Luke's Gospel, then we probably have truly forgiven.

My counselor was a great help here. She sympathized with the pain of rejection I was experiencing but affirmed me in my roles of daughter, sister, sister-in-law, mother, and grandmother. No one could take those honorable positions away from me. They are positions of spiritual power and authority whereby I can pray for my relatives out of a heart of forgiveness and love.

I began to pray in earnest with great love for these relatives who had rejected me. I prayed for everything I wanted for myself. I prayed for these relatives to have financial wisdom, peace, security, and prosperity. I prayed for excellent health and divine healing. I prayed for them to have deep intimate walks with God and to hear His voice. I prayed for them and their families to have wonderful Christian fellowship all their lives and for great rewards in heaven. I prayed that they would be pleasing to God, bring glory to Him with their lives, and be greatly used in His kingdom.

I am sharing all the details of my prayers with you to help you begin to pray for your enemies. It is one of the most effective tools I have discovered for the deep healing of emotional wounds and for achieving true forgiveness from our hearts, as Christ instructs us.

After my divorce, one relative did not speak to me or communicate with me in any way for over three years. I studied Monica and began to pray for him the way she prayed for her son. I prayed for him to come to know God. I still pray in this way, but today I also choose to love and accept him just as he is. I will always pray for him, but now I trust that God is working behind the scenes in his life. God knows what He is doing. God is God and He is sovereign.

After three and a half years, this relative spoke

to me and was kind, and I will forever be indebted to Monica. Her endurance helped me keep going. All I really have to do is to continue to have faith, hope, and love.

I was impressed with Augustine's warnings about secular education. My former husband and I, while raising our children, worried that some schools would have negative effects on them. We homeschooled them when we could. We sent them to Christian schools when we were able. We treated them each as individuals and tried to make the best decisions for each one of them.

I loved homeschooling and found we all bonded spiritually when we were at home together. The homeschooling community in Dallas also offered great opportunities for sports and socialization. The academic subjects were well presented by various homeschooling curriculums. The fellowship among homeschooling families was in itself worth the whole effort. All of our children finished college and went on to get further degrees. All are independent and successful adults now.

Let's Talk

1. What impresses you most about Monica, her life, and her character?
2. What do you think of the difficulties she had with her marriage? What do you think of the advice she gave to married women who were her contemporaries?
3. Describe a situation you know about where children are rejecting their parents.
4. What Scriptures come to mind when you think of Monica and her life and prayers?
5. What did you know about Saint Augustine and Monica before reading this?
6. What impresses you most about Saint Augustine?
7. Do you know any parents who have suffered rejection from their children and afterward enjoyed reconciliation?

Five

Barbara Johnson:
Joy in Grief

B arbara and two of her sons were driving up
to the church retreat on a mountain in the
dark when they saw a man stumbling around
in the middle of the road. He looked as if he had
been severely injured. His head was bleeding and
he moved in a way that indicated that he could
not see. His clothing was torn and disheveled. He
looked like a man on the doorstep of death. Then
Barbara recognized the clothing—the man stumbling and bleeding in the dark was her husband!
He was indeed stumbling around in the darkness,
injured and bleeding. She and her sons were aston-
ished, distressed, and filled with fear. Her husband
had gone up early to help prepare for a Christian
retreat. Barbara had followed with her two younger
sons.

Barbara Johnson had a great deal of emotional

pain in her life. She was also a fabulous and humorous speaker. Her trademark was that in the midst of terrible pain and suffering, she looked for and found joy, laughter, and upbeat wisdom.

Before his accident, Barbara and her engineer husband, Bill, were a successful, happy American family in California. They had four sons, all of whom were Christians. The boys were stable, upright, and normal. There was no indication that tragedy crouched around the corner.

Their family looked like the American dream until her husband had the accident. In her first book, *Where Does a Mother go to Resign?* she chronicled her "valley experience."[35] The terrible car accident left her husband blind and crippled for many months. Then one son died in Vietnam, another son died on a highway in the Yukon, and another son disappeared into the lifestyle of homosexuals for the better part of eleven years.

The first blow came in 1966 when she and her husband were scheduled to be counselors at a youth retreat in the San Gabriel Mountains in California. As described at the opening of this chapter, on the road up the mountain, Bill's car hit some debris and overturned. Their two oldest sons, Steve and Tim, were going on the bus to the camp with the youth group. Bill had gone up to help prepare for

---

[35] Barbara Johnson, *Stick a Geranium in Your Hat and Be Happy!* Nashville: W Publishing Group, a division of Thomas Nelson, Inc., 2004), xvii.

the retreat. Barbara and her two younger sons, Larry and Barney, found Bill bleeding and unrecognizable in the middle of the road with head injuries that exposed part of his brain. The doctors told her he would probably live the rest of his life as a vegetable—without vision and without memory.[36]

Barbara worked hard for months getting help from the Veterans Administration, Social Security Disability, Aid for the Blind, and insurance policies. Just as she finished the work with all of these agencies, God miraculously healed her husband! Not overnight but little by little, Bill's vision returned, his memory returned, and he wanted to go back to work.

She said getting off of all the agencies was as complicated and as difficult as it had been getting help from them! It was hard to convince the government workers that a miracle had occurred, but they could not deny that Bill could see, hear, think, and work once again. The hardest agency to convince was the Department of Motor Vehicles. They didn't believe that a man who had been blind and had brain damage and seizures could ever drive again. It took months to convince them.

Meanwhile, their second son, Steve, along with several buddies, had joined the marines after he finished his senior year in high school.[37] He was a Christian and was shipped off to Vietnam in 1968.

[36] Johnson, *Stick a Geranium in Your Hat and Be Happy!*, 19.
[37] Johnson, *Stick a Geranium in Your Hat and Be Happy!*, 21.

Barbara was not happy with his going but knew she needed to support a son who was becoming a man. His letters showed that his faith in God was deepening as his buddies dropped in battle all around him. He himself was killed on July 28, 1968, and three days later a car marked "US Marines" drove up to the Johnsons' home.[38] Two young marines in full dress uniform came to tell Barbara and Bill that Steve and his entire platoon had been killed in a battle near Da Nang.

Barbara had to go to the morgue to identify her son to comply with the law, which stipulated that if someone dies in a foreign country, the remains have to be identified. She had a hard time identifying him as he had lain face down in a rice paddy for two days. But she finally decided it must be Steve, so they had a memorial service for him. She was sure that the worst of their suffering was over. She considered the one son they had lost to be their deposit in heaven, and her husband, Bill, was recovering.

Their oldest son, Tim, was normally not a bundle of fun. A quiet and melancholy young man, he took a trip to Alaska with a friend when he was twenty-three. He called collect to tell his parents that he had had a fabulous spiritual experience in Canada and that his life had completely changed. He was joyful, boisterous, and optimistic on the

---

[38] Johnson, *Stick a Geranium in Your Hat and Be Happy!*, 22.

phone. He couldn't wait to come home and tell his parents about his new spirituality. Barbara and Bill eagerly awaited his return at dinner with their two remaining sons, Larry and Barney.[39]

But a telephone call from the Canadian police interrupted their happy dinner. Drunk boys in a three-ton truck had crossed the center line, hit Tim's Volkswagen head on, and killed Tim and his friend immediately.[40]

They never heard Tim tell them his story. Barbara says that the pain of having to go to the morgue a second time to identify the remains of a beloved son was more than any mother should have to bear. The pastor from the church in Alaska where their son had been transformed came to the memorial service. He was a comfort, but now they had two sons sent ahead as deposits in heaven.

Then Barbara developed adult-onset diabetes. This was a blow, with a lot of fear and inconvenience and dramatic negative imaginations involved, but she confides that the greatest pain and suffering came from the discovery that one of their remaining sons had become a practicing homosexual. This should not happen in a Christian family, she argued with God. She was very angry with God and didn't believe her family deserved such rough treatment.

Barbara was very open in her books about her

[39] Johnson, *Stick a Geranium in Your Hat and Be Happy!*, 25.
[40] Johnson, *Stick a Geranium in Your Hat and Be Happy!*, 25.

emotions. She reacted in total anger and disgust when she found out that Larry was a practicing homosexual. She alienated her son by her behavior and laid the groundwork for his total rejection of their family. Later, after sitting in her bedroom counting roses on the wallpaper for what felt like an eternity, she decided to stop focusing on her own pain and help others get through theirs.

Barbara Johnson started Spatula Ministries, helping other Christians and parents in pain. They called it Spatula Ministries because she said they were dedicated to helping scrape parents off of the ceiling when they discovered their children in the homosexual lifestyle. Some parents had children who were active homosexuals; others had lost their children through death or desertion. Barbara opened her heart to any parent who was suffering on behalf of a child. She taught that pain in this life is inevitable, but that misery is optional.[41] She decided to spend the rest of her life looking for humor and joy. She had an entire room in their home dedicated to joy and humor.

When we are going through pain and heartache, we often forget how to laugh. Yet laughter is one of the best medicines with healing qualities. Some think it is not appropriate to be happy or joyful when we are faced with heartbreaking issues. But Barbara Johnson showed we can still smile and

---

[41] Johnson, *Stick a Geranium in Your Hat and Be Happy!*, 1.

enjoy life in spite of our difficulties. She collected joy thoughts and uplifting poems and quotations. Her books are filled with loving, hopeful ideas, such as:

Acceptance

> Acceptance is the answer to all my problems today.
> When I am disturbed, it is because I find some person,
> place, thing, or situation – some fact of my life – unacceptable to me, and I can find no serenity until I accept
> that person, place, thing, or situation as being exactly the way it is supposed to be at this moment. Nothing, absolutely nothing, happens in God's world by mistake.
> Unless I accept life completely on life's terms, I cannot be happy.
> I need to concentrate not so much on what needs to be changed in the world as on what needs to be changed in me and in my attitudes.
> —Source unknown

We are so blessed when we are reminded of the truth that God loves us and is working everything out for our good and His glory as is promised in Romans 8:28. Jesus told His disciples they would find joy after their sufferings: "Truly, truly, I say to you, that you will weep and lament, but the world will rejoice; you will grieve, but your grief will be turned into joy. Whenever a woman is in labor she has pain, because her hour has come; but when she gives birth to the child, she no longer remembers the anguish because of the joy that a child has been born into the world. Therefore you too have grief now; but I will see you again, and your heart will rejoice, and no one will take your joy away from you" (John 16:20–22 NASB).

The health benefits of positive emotions are noted in Scripture: "A joyful heart is good medicine, But a broken spirit dries up the bones" (Prov. 17:22 NASB). Psalm 30:5 says that "weeping endures for a night, but joy comes in the morning."

Sometimes it seems like the night of suffering lasts for years and feels like a lifetime, but Jesus's joy is always available if we turn things over to Him and wait for Him.

Getting Personal

I don't know of any pain greater than the emotional pain of being rejected by a close and loved family member. The relatives I have already spoken about, whom I love dearly, decided I was to be an outcast from their families. This caused physical pain of heartache that continued unabated for weeks and months. I know what it is like to have emotional pain that just will not go away. I tried praying for them, for great blessings on their family, and tried to work through forgiveness in the best ways I knew. There was very little relief. I tried to think about other things and tried to stay busy, but the default thought processes were set on the rejection. Not only was I rejected, but my character and sanity were questioned. I tried not to dwell on the situation, but every time I turned around, there was my broken heart staring at me.

I tried to comfort myself by assuring myself that Jesus Himself had great trouble from His family members and was vilified and misunderstood by many of them. Scripture indicates that they thought He was out of His mind. He simply ignored them, but Scripture also tells us that He was a man of sorrows and acquainted with grief.

Prosperity preaching, modern advertising, and our own desires for happiness and freedom from pain lead us to believe that we should not suffer. However, on this sinful planet and in this broken world, we will all experience many forms of suffering. For those of us who are Christians, we want to go through our suffering in a way that pleases God and brings Him glory. Jesus's example was given to us in First Peter 2:19–21: "For it is commendable if a man bears up under the pain of unjust suffering because he is conscious of God . . . But if you suffer for doing good and you endure it, this is commendable before God. To this you were called, because Christ suffered for you, leaving you an example that you should follow in His steps."

The chapter goes on to say how when they hurled insults at Him, Jesus did not respond or react but entrusted Himself to Him who judges fairly. Read that passage again very carefully. We are called to follow Jesus and to conform our behavior to His example. If we are attacked, rejected, or maligned and we do not defend ourselves, we are entrusting our reputation and our very lives to God, our loving heavenly Father. Here we must follow the leading of the Holy Spirit in how much, if at all, we should defend ourselves. The passage talks about bearing up under the pain of unjust suffering and enduring it. Here is where our flesh will react with righteous indignation. It is so unfair! We did nothing wrong! We are innocent, and perhaps we have done great kind and loving deeds that are rewarded with hatred and hostility. It is then that we must remind ourselves of how much Jesus suffered on our behalf and how much we want to honor Him and bring glory to His name. Sometimes we simply must endure for a long while.

Another particularly painful experience that I suffered through was being falsely accused by several family members. For more than a decade I was gossiped about and slandered by various relatives. These accusing persons were able to convince other family members that I was guilty. The result was that I was scapegoated and virtually driven out of my family of origin. A few relatives still believed in me but were afraid to speak up in my defense. If they did speak up, they were attacked and ostracized.

The biggest challenge was the temptation to sin and harbor bitterness, resentment, and unforgiveness in my heart because the offenses were unjustified, cruel, and ongoing. With each new untruth told, I had to make the decision to forgive. Many Christian teachers have stressed that forgiveness is a choice, an act of the will, not a feeling. You may still feel hurt even after you have truly forgiven. Each decision to forgive again restarts the process of forgiveness. I had to start anew praying for my enemies.

I don't believe it brings glory to God to recite all the details of these injustices in this book. Just know that the offenses were deep, very personal, and struck at the core of my integrity and Christian character. I was able to comfort myself in that Jesus had also suffered from gossip, slander, misunderstandings, and false accusations.

When I was suffering emotionally from my divorce, a friend sent me Barbara Johnson's book, *I'm So Glad You Told Me What I Didn't Wanna Hear.*[42] Her book, with the stories and letters from parents who had lost a child to death or homosexuality, comforted me. I was thankful that my four children were still alive and living uneventfully. Some

[42] Barbara Johnson, *I'm So Glad You Told Me What I Didn't Wanna Hear* (Dallas: Word Publishing, 1996).

of my family relationships were strained because of the divorce, but hope was rampant.

It has always helped me to hear how other Christians have dealt with difficulties and overcome them. A kindred spirit unites people who have suffered. My pain came from a divorce after almost thirty-three years of what had been a solid Christian family. Reading about parents who had suffered more than I had and who had problems and issues I considered worse than mine, somehow helped me. I don't know if this is good or bad, but it helped me. It reminds me of the person who felt sorry for himself for having no shoes until he met a man who had no feet.

During this time God comforted me with a passage from Isaiah 48:10–11: "Behold, I have refined you, but not as silver, I have tested you in the furnace of affliction; For My own sake, for My own sake I will act. For how can My name be profaned? My glory I will not give to another."

This passage comforted me because I was not the only one whom God loved and yet had allowed to go through the furnace of affliction. A furnace burns off anything that is not core to the metal in the furnace, so perhaps God was using these trials to refine me and to deliver me from sins, habits, or thoughts that did not please Him.

By the time I read her books, Barbara Johnson had already died. She was diagnosed in 2001 with a brain tumor and fought central nervous system lymphoma until her death in 2007 at the age of seventy-nine. Her husband, Bill, had gone to heaven three years before she entered into glory. I never heard her in person.

Not to worry. I found her on YouTube and watched her presentations over and over again. She was delightful, inspiring, warm, and wonderful. She truly had a gift for humor and her stories took my mind off of my problems.

It used to puzzle me that Jesus told His disciples right before He was crucified that He was about to be glorified in John 17:5. But we are told in Hebrews 12:2 that "for the joy set before him He endured the cross." Our sufferings are an opportunity for our lives to bring glory to God. When we go through difficulties with love, joy, peace, patience, goodness, kindness, gentleness, and self-control, and with a thankful attitude, it brings glory to Him.

Robert Morgan, in his excellent book, *The Red Sea Rules*,[43] says that when facing trials we should be more concerned with how we can bring glory to God than with our own relief. A friend gave me this book when I went home to New Orleans to live with my parents. The first rule is that you are exactly where God wants you to be. This was

---

[43] Robert Morgan, *The Red Sea Rules* (Nashville: W Publishing Group, a division of Thomas Nelson, Inc., 2014), 19.

a great comfort to me when my marriage had just broken up. How could I be where God wanted me to be? I had to accept this by faith. The second rule is to be more concerned for God's glory than for our relief. If we go through trials and suffering with a good attitude, it brings glory to God.

Barbara Johnson would not have had the opportunity to help so many people and to be used by God to bless others if she had not gone through what she did. No one would wish pain and suffering on others, but when God works through our sorrows to bring glory to Himself, He builds our faith and gives us an intimate knowledge of Himself.

Let's Talk

1. What relief have you found in the midst of suffering? How have you experienced joy in the middle of trials? How have you experienced humor? Why did Barbara look for or expect joy in the midst of her suffering?

2. Can you describe a time of suffering in your own life where you saw God bring great good out of the situation at a later time?

3. Why do you think Christians in America might not want to admit that suffering is a part of the Christian life?

4. What do you think Barbara's motivation was for helping others find joy in their suffering? What do you think her reward was?

5. How do you think Barbara's husband reacted to her ministry? Do you think he was an important part of it?

6. What Scriptures come to mind when you think of Barbara Johnson?

7. Have you lost children or do you know people who have? How did you or they deal with the loss? If you haven't experienced it, how do you think you would deal with such a loss?

Six

Hannah Whitall Smith: The Secret of Happiness

H annah gasped as she heard the news that her husband was being unfaithful with another woman. How could this happen? They were leaders in the Christian movement of their time. God had anointed and blessed their ministry. They had vowed when they were married to keep themselves only for each other. Her husband knew the Lord and was devoted to God. How could this have happened? She felt betrayed.

Hannah Tatum Whitall Smith was born on February 7, 1832, in Philadelphia. She was a dedicated Christian and a popular lay speaker and author in the United States. Hannah was a part of the Holiness movement and the Higher Life movement in the United Kingdom and Ireland[44] as well as in

---

[44] Hannah Whitall Smith, *The Unselfishness of God and How I Discovered It* (Tentmaker Ministries & Publications, 2011), originally published by Fleming H. Revell Company in 1903.

the United States. She loved God and was faithful to Him even when her husband deserted her.

John Wesley, founder of the Methodist church in the late seventeen hundreds in England, had urged his followers to aspire to holiness in their Christian life and laid the foundation for the later Holiness movements. Another prominent belief among these disciples was that a second filling of the Holy Spirit or a second baptism enabled Christians to live a higher life free from the compulsion to sin.

Hannah received a good and godly education at the Quaker school of Miss Longstroth in Philadelphia and in 1851 married John Smith. She conducted Bible classes for women at their home in Philadelphia. She offered her home as a headquarters for various religious projects and movements. From 1873 to 1874, she and her husband sailed to England where they conducted a series of religious meetings.

A serious and mature Christian woman, Hannah preached what was then called the Higher Life. These methods and practices were also known as "The Deeper Life." She called it "the walk of faith" or "sanctification."[45] Hannah is most widely known today as the author of *The Christian's Secret of a Happy Life*. It is still a popular Christian book and

[45] Hannah Whitall Smith, *The Christian's Secret of a Happy Life* (Grand Rapids: Revell, a division of Baker Publishing Group, 1952), 26, originally published 1886.

is a good defense of and explanation of her teachings about the Higher Life.

In her book, Hannah compares life to an underwater scene where we are protected by a large and indestructible fishnet. We are there underwater, protected while sharks, electric eels, stingrays, and harpoons come at us to injure us. She says God's love and protection are like the fishnet. Bullets, harpoons, and dangerous fish cannot break through. However, every once in a while God makes an opening and carefully allows a trial to pass through the net and into our lives. He only allows certain trials that have a specific purpose to benefit us or help us grow to be more like Christ.

Hannah wrote that if we can look at life this way, and truly believe and trust in the loving providence of our heavenly Father, then we can take everything that happens as a direct love gift straight from the Father's hand.

Hannah and her husband, John Smith, were a celebrated team in the beginning of their marriage and ministry. They were Christian leaders in nineteenth-century America and were admired. Having been from a well-known Quaker family of New Jersey may have helped open doors for Hannah and her husband. She and her husband together lived and taught Keswick theology.

The basic principle of Keswick theology is that a Christian who is born again needs the influence of the Holy Spirit to live a life consistent with the Bible. The Keswick followers taught that all Christians should experience continued sanctification and be baptized in or filled with the Holy Spirit. The Keswick teachings held that we could live a higher life or a deeper life than that which a carnal or "baby Christian" gets stuck in. This theology was based on a book by William Boardman, *The Higher Christian Life,* published in 1858. It was part of the Holiness movement that originated in England.

It seems that Hannah and John Smith were on the edges of a type of charismatic movement where spiritual experiences and mysticism were prevalent. Perhaps her husband fell into the extremes of emotionalism. We never know all the deep feelings and issues a Christian who falls into sin struggles with. Nevertheless, Hannah's husband, after some years of ministry, gave in to temptation and became involved with other women while they were still married. Hannah and John separated. Hannah remained faithful to her marriage vows and remained single and chaste. She was a true "covenant keeper."[46] She continued to write and speak and God continued to anoint and bless her ministry. She wrote in her book *Religious Fanaticism,*[47] "A quiet

[46] Covenant Keepers is a ministry of people who stay true to their marriage vows even after separation or divorce, https://www.covenantkeepersinc.org/.

[47] Hannah Whitall Smith, *Religious fanaticism: Extracts from the papers of Hannah Whitall Smith* (New York: AMS Press, 1976).

steadfast holding of the human will to the will of God and a peaceful resting in His love and care is of infinitely greater value in the religious life than the most intense emotions or the most wonderful experiences that have ever been known by the greatest mystic of them all."

Her husband never came back to his senses and went to live in England. Hannah continued to minister and remained faithful to God.

In *The Christian's Secret of a Happy Life*, Hannah explains that there are two parts to this walk of faith: man's part and God's part. Man's part is to trust God, and God's part is to do the work of sanctification in the Christian's heart.

Even though Christian mores in the late eighteen hundreds were stronger in society than they are today, I am sure Hannah was tempted to enjoy male company. She may have had male friends, but due to the influence and admiration she was awarded by her followers, I am sure that they were only friends.

The Quakers shaped her early life and doctrine, but she was also moved by the Wesleyan doctrine of sanctification. She was involved with the Plymouth Brethren and Methodist revivalists, but her teachings reflect her own personal struggles to walk closely with God.

Hannah was on the cutting edge of reform for her time. She participated in the Women's Suffrage movement as well as the Temperance movement. As such, she held strong feminist views, which went against the abuses and excesses of the patriarchal family structures of the nineteenth century.

I found her book *The Christian's Secret to a Happy Life* to be well reasoned and clearly presented. Her book outlines the methods she found most helpful in understanding God and living in close fellowship with Him. In 1888, she moved with her remaining family to London, England. She died there on May 1, 1911, at the age of seventy-nine.

Getting Personal

One of the practices that brought me great healing and comfort was taught by Merlin Carothers in many of his books. *Prison to Praise*[48] is his most famous. In these inspiring books he teaches that we can bring God into any situation by praise and thanksgiving. He goes so far as to thank God *for* the difficult situation. Ephesians 5:20 points us to this practice. This is hard to do and does not make sense to our natural minds, but it is very powerful and effective. Doing so brings God into the situation in a mighty way. Romans 8:28 promises us that in everything God works for the good of those who love Him and are called according to His purposes. Praising and thanking God in any situation is biblical.

[48] Merlin R. Carothers, *Prison to Praise* (Escondido, California: 1970).

The greatest tragedy in the history of mankind was the crucifixion of the Lord of glory on the cross, yet out of that came our salvation. God can bring good out of any situation or circumstance or tragedy if we seek Him and turn it over to Him. This takes surrender and faith, but God is always working in every situation for our good according to Romans 8:28.

Let's Talk

1. Had you heard of Hannah Whitall Smith before reading this? What do you think of her life and her witness?
2. What Scriptures come to mind when you think of her life?
3. Can you share with others any knowledge of the Quakers and how they worship?
4. Have you had experiences with the Holy Spirit that you can talk about?
5. How would you describe what was called the "deeper life?"
6. Do you know anyone whose spouse has done to them what Hannah's husband did to her? How did they react? Were they able to forgive and go on with God?

Seven

Madame de Lafayette: A Revolutionary Woman

The door to the dank, dark cell opened slowly as a lovely, gracious well-dressed woman carefully stepped into the prison cell. It was underground and only a small barred window at the top of the wall let in some sunlight. In it a man sat in tattered clothing, sick and famished. Adrienne de Lafayette was shocked to see her husband so emaciated and poorly clothed, sitting amidst the filth of the Austrian prison. She had persuaded the German emperor to allow her and her two daughters to go and live with the Marquis de Lafayette in his prison cell. The teenage girls were put in another cell but were allowed to join their parents during the day.[49]

---

[49] The info for Madame de Lafayette is from various sources the author studied and taught on and from public knowledge on Madame de Lafayette.

Adrienne de Lafayette, wife of the famous general and American Revolutionary war hero Marquis de Lafayette, was a brave and committed Christian woman. Born into a wealthy family of French nobility, and marrying one of the wealthiest men in France, she had great resources.

Adrienne de Lafayette lived during the time of the French Revolution and was threatened with the loss of her life by guillotine. The nobles were all hoarded together in a building in Paris and the revolutionists came daily to take certain of them to their deaths. Marie Adrienne Francois de Noailles rose to the occasion and displayed true nobility as her mother, grandmother, aunts, and sister were all put to death by the French mobs. Miraculously, her life was spared.

Once during the revolution, Adrienne had to travel across the country by stagecoach with her two daughters. She did not know if she would be stopped and detained because she was nobility. She drew on her Christian faith and trusted the Lord to protect her, which He did. She was very brave and her faith was the foundation for her courage. Adrienne had been raised in the Roman Catholic Church and remained true to her deepest Christian convictions all her life. She was a shining example of humility, graciousness, loyalty, and devotion to her family.

She was born Adrienne in her family home in

Paris on November 2, 1759. At age fourteen she was married by the arrangement made by the authorities in both families to the Marquis de Lafayette when he was sixteen. He was an orphan who was inheriting one of the largest estates in France, with an annual income of almost $2 million. Early marriages and arranged marriages were common in her time. Her mother was careful to arrange a marriage where she approved of the young man. Young Lafayette was polite, polished, and handsome. He was very well thought of by those who were prominent in French society and was well behaved. At first, he did not have the dedicated faith that Adrienne had, but he grew in his faith as his life unfolded.

Adrienne was delighted with her new husband and thought he was the most handsome and attractive man she had ever seen. She fell madly in love with him and remained that way for the rest of her life. For his part, Lafayette was touched by the attentions of some of the women of the very immoral and materialistic court life of Louis the XVI. Adrienne could not have been happy about the temptations thrown in the path of her handsome husband. Unfortunately, the immoral court life was so established and so accepted that there was not much she could do to counter the situations her husband faced. She continued to love and pray devotedly for her husband. She was loyal to him and faithful to her traditional Catholic Christian upbringing.

Adrienne was one of those unusual women who, while wealthy and well-born, continued to advance in virtue and true nobility of character. She started businesses for the poverty-stricken peasants around the chateau her family owned. Her mother had been determined that her daughters received a solid, doctrinally sound Christian education. Adrienne had made her faith her own and desired to grow in character as a dedicated Christian woman. She surely must have prayed for her husband. It was rumored that he was interested in a woman at court who turned him down. Perhaps Adrienne's prayers protected him.

Her young husband was not only well-built and good-looking, but he was also very idealistic. Having been raised by his grandmother and aunts on stories of family, especially military heroics, he discovered within himself a passion for liberty, which became the driving force of his life. This passion for liberty and freedom for all men and women without the constraints of the monarchist court life made him sympathetic to the peasants. He loved liberty enough to sail across the Atlantic at his own expense and to fight for America's freedom from England. He became close friends with General George Washington. Washington admired his courage and his devotion to liberty. Lafayette was instrumental in helping the French decide to come into the war on America's side. Without their navy and financial help, we might not have won the War of Independence from England.

In England, Lafayette had met some of the military men who would serve as generals fighting for England against the American colonies in the American Revolution. His father had died in battle against the British, and he wanted revenge. He eventually found a satisfying irony in fighting against them in America. He caught the vision of liberty in America and left his beautiful young wife expecting their second baby to sail to what is now the United States to help the young country win independence from Great Britain.

Lafayette's king, Louis XVI, was not at all pleased with his departure for America and tried to stop him. But Lafayette was determined and escaped to Spain to sail to America from there. He took a chance that the king's soldiers might have pursued and arrested him, but he escaped.

Adrienne was as devoted to the concept of liberty as her husband, a truly supportive wife. A devout Catholic, she undoubtedly understood the relation between true liberty and the freedom with which we are "endowed by our Creator" as an "inalienable right." She suffered greatly emotionally while her husband was in America. The death of their infant daughter Henriette while he was gone also caused

Lafayette much grief, and he lamented the fact that he could not be there to comfort Adrienne.

Adrienne's greatest demonstration of love and devotion was her decision to join her husband after the war when he was imprisoned in Prussia. He had been imprisoned because while he was nobility, he had identified with the peasants and supported some of their causes. He especially wanted France to be a constitutional monarchy that would uphold and defend liberty and the rights of man. The monarchs of Europe feared that he would start revolutions in their countries and the safest thing was to just put him in prison.

Adrienne begged the emperor of Germany for mercy and he gave her permission to take their two daughters and join her husband in prison. The emperor might have wanted to do more, but due to political pressures he could not grant the marquis complete liberty. Adrienne and their daughters took care of Lafayette while imprisoned for two years.

All of Adrienne's money and possessions were confiscated, and she never recovered her health from her prison sojourn, but she did secure her husband's release after two years. It is doubtful that he would have been released if she had not joined him and kept his plight in front of the world leaders of her time.

Adrienne told her friends and family that she

loved being in prison with him because it was the first time she had him all to herself. He adored her after that episode. Perhaps he came to faith in Jesus Christ as his Savior in response to the love and care his wife lavished on him in prison.

After Lafayette was released from prison, Adrienne worked to regain some of the properties that had been taken from them. Much had been sold and could not be recovered, but her political skills and business sense helped recover enough for the family to live on. Adrienne died early at the age of forty-eight, but the marquis remained faithful to her memory all the rest of his life. He died in his mid-seventies, surrounded by his loving family, with a miniature of his faithful wife clutched in his hand.

Getting Personal

I grew up with an appreciation of our country, our founding fathers, and the biblical principles that our country was founded upon. I have great affection for General and Madame de Lafayette and am grateful for the part they played in America's struggle for independence from Great Britain. When we see countries today where freedom is curtailed or nonexistent, we can be thankful for all the men and women who made our freedoms possible.

Having been involved in politics, I am amazed at how Madame de Lafayette stood up for her husband with the king and the court and would not give up until she had recovered a good deal of their land.

If I am tempted to feel sorry for myself because of my circumstances, I remember Adrienne in prison with her beloved husband. I cannot imagine living in such squalid circumstances with her two teenage daughters, not knowing if they would ever be released. She was a courageous woman of great faith whose memory is an inspiration to us all.

Let's Talk

1. What do you know about the French Revolution?

2. How do you think Adrienne felt when her husband was sought after by so many women in the French court? How would you have responded?

3. What do you think of Adrienne's loyalty to her husband? Her joining him in prison?

4. What Scriptures come to mind when you consider Adrienne's life?

5. What do you know about the great part her husband played in the American Revolution?

6. What do you know about the French court of her time? What do you admire most in Adrienne's life and character?

Eight

Madame Guyon: Imprisoned for Her Faith

Madame Guyon was led by a large and strong guard to a small room in the dark and lonely French Bastille prison. Only her loyal personal maid was allowed to go with her. She had humbled herself before the Catholic theologians who were drilling her about her writings on prayer. She had enjoyed great success and admiration in teaching ordinary men and women how to pray intimately to their God. She acquiesced and agreed not to teach any more of her deep spiritual truths, but the men were adamant. The theologians believed that she must be punished for standing up against the church. They ultimately put her in the Bastille for three years.[50]

---

[50] The info for Madame Guyon is from various sources the author studied and taught on and from public knowledge on Madame Guyon.

Jeanne-Marie Bouvier de la Motte-Guyon, also known as Madame Guyon, was born in April 1648 in Montargis, France, and lived mostly in France until she died in Blois on June 9, 1717. Madame Guyon was born to very religious parents and had a pious upbringing. She wanted to become a nun, but her parents denied her this avenue, arranging a marriage between their beloved daughter and a very wealthy and prominent French bachelor. The marriage was not destined to be a happy one, but her parents had no way of knowing this. Her father adored her and arranged for her to visit his home many times. She may have told them something of her tribulations, because she writes in her auto-biography that the family thought that she should have stood up for herself more.

After her parents denied Jeanne's wish to become a nun, the arranged marriage they had planned for her took place when she was only fifteen. Her husband, Jacques Guyon, was thirty-eight years old when they married. He was not an ideal husband. He was either unable or unwilling to protect her from ill-treatment by his mother and the household servants where she had to live.

Miserable in her situation, Madame Guyon turned dramatically to Jesus Christ Himself. She learned to pray Scripture, taking one verse at a time and turning it over and over in her mind. She would draw all she could from every word of the verse and pray however the Holy Spirit led her. Jesus came alive for her and helped her bear the cruelty of her married life. He gave her unexpected and otherworldly joy as she raised her children. As she grew in her faith, she naturally began to share her experiences with others and was regarded as an enthusiastic mystic. She rejoiced in the presence and love of her Lord even in the middle of arduous circumstances.

During her marriage, her misery was increased by the deaths of her mother, a half-sister, one of her sons, a daughter, and finally her own father. Madame Guyon's faith grew stronger during these trials. She believed that God had a purpose and a perfect plan for her life and that He would bless her in her suffering. Her search for a deep and intimate relationship with God sustained her during her most challenging days. Turning to Him, she was able to hold her head high and become the woman God created her to be.

Madame Guyon is most famous for her teachings that people can have a deep, intimate spiritual relationship with God through Jesus Christ on their own through prayer without having to go through a Catholic priest. Her teachings did not sit well with the Roman Catholic Church of her time and she ended up in prison several times from 1695 through 1703. The church was upset with her for publishing a book entitled *A Short and Easy*

Method of Prayer.[51] She was imprisoned even after retracting her books, accepting Catholic theology, and agreeing not to spread her beliefs further.

Another book by Madame Guyon is titled (translated from the French) *Christian and Spiritual Letters on Various Subjects Regarding the Interior Life of the Spirit and the Christian Life.*[52]

Madame Guyon was blessed to be the daughter of Claude Bouvier, a well-to-do and deeply pious Roman Catholic. Her father adored her and was very kind and generous to her. She always felt that her mother preferred her other siblings to herself. She was educated partly in convents and was influenced by the writings of Saint Francis de Sales, a Roman Catholic saint. Saint Francis de Sales lived from 1567 to 1622 and had been the Bishop of Geneva. He was known for his strong faith and loving approach to the divisions resulting from the growth of Protestantism in his diocese. He preached about the love, kindness, and compassion of God. He believed in the education of the laity and wrote *Introduction to the Devout Life*[53] especially for them. He was called "the gentleman saint" because of his love, patience, and gentleness.

[51] Madame Jeanne Guyon, *A Short and Easy Method of Prayer* (CreateSpace Publishing, 2010).

[52] Madame Jeanne Guyon, *Christian and Spiritual Letters on Various Subjects Regarding the Interior Life of the Spirit and the Christian Life* (London, MDCCLXVII).

[53] Francis de Sales, *Introduction to the Devout Life* (New York: Harper & Row, 1966).

In 1676, after twelve years of marriage, Madame Guyon's husband died, leaving her a very wealthy twenty-eight-year-old widow. During their problematic marriage, she had borne her husband five children, three of whom had survived. She had done her best to bring them up in the nurture and admonition of the Lord, as we are exhorted to do in Ephesians 5. One son who had mistreated her turned around and became loyal to her at the end of her life. He went to live with her when she was exiled from Paris and was with her through the remaining years of her life.

Among those who loved her for her piety and her love of God was Francois Fenelon. Fenelon was born Francois de Salignac de la Mothe-Fenelon in 1651 and lived until 1715, when he died at the age of sixty-four. He became a well-known and beloved French Catholic Archbishop, theologian, poet, priest, and writer. His works are still valued by Christians today. A well-educated young man, he was born into a family that had produced prominent clergy and statesmen for centuries. He studied theology in Paris and showed such promise that he was invited to give a public sermon when he was only fifteen. At age twenty-four he was ordained as a priest.

Today he is best remembered for his *The Adventures of Telemachus*, which was first published in 1699. Telemachus was Odysseus's son and his adventures were a vehicle for Fenelon to question the doctrine of the divine right of kings to rule. The book caused a great stir when it first became popular. Of course, kings and their royal families disapproved.

In early 1679, the Archbishop of Paris appointed Fenelon to be the director of Nouvelles-Catholiques, a Parisian community of young Huguenot (French Protestant) girls who had been taken from their families and were being prepared to join the Roman Catholic Church. Later Fenelon was chosen by Louis XIV to preach to the Huguenots against Protestantism. In 1689, he was named tutor to the Dauphin's eldest son, the seven-year-old Duke of Burgundy, who was second in line for the throne. However, when Louis XIV caught wind of his Telemachus attack on the divine right of kings, Fenelon was removed as a tutor.

As Fenelon's reputation and influence grew, he was sought after by socially prominent families for advice. He urged them to educate their daughters as well as their sons. He wanted the women to be able to recognize and refute heresies. He wrote an article, "Traits De L'education Des Filles" (Matters Concerning the Education of Young Women) regarding the education of young girls. This work was ahead of its time, but it greatly prepared Fenelon to be an encouragement and an ally to Madame Guyon.

In 1688, Fenelon met Madame Guyon, who was well received at the time in prominent social circles. Fenelon and Guyon were cousins. Historians believe that he taught and encouraged her. He recognized the reality of her relationship with God and was impressed with her sincerity and her deep understanding of spirituality. Through this friendship, Madame Guyon's influence increased with those who were powerful at court. When she was attacked for her beliefs, he defended her.

Madame Guyon was questioned by an ecclesiastical commission set up by the Roman Catholic Church. They studied her books and gave a report that pointed to parts of her beliefs that did not square with Catholic doctrine. She immediately submitted to their authority. Although she acquiesced, they studied her writings a second time. Fenelon defended her and said she had already been scrutinized once and that she had agreed with the commission. Why attack her again? But they did and they found more errors and objectionable beliefs.

Tragically, she was jailed for her beliefs in 1695. In 1699, she was arrested again even though she had signed retractions of her works and promised not to continue to spread her beliefs. Louis XIV and others were afraid at this time of the growth of a form of Christianity called Quietism. Madame Guyon's beliefs and practices were too close to

Quietism for their comfort. Quietism emphasized meditation and contemplation and was deemed a heresy by the Roman Catholic Church for its practice of inward quietness seeking to experience oneness with God. The king and the priests thought it fostered pacifism and spiritual indolence. It was condemned as heresy by Pope Innocent XI in 1687. Some historians believe that the church simply did not want to lose power and control of its members by allowing them to have a deep intimate relationship with God apart from the services of a Catholic priest.

Madame Guyon was ultimately imprisoned in the Bastille, a huge fortress used as a state prison by the kings of France. Louis XIV used it to detain members of the social upper class who had angered or crossed him, including many French Protestants. Her loyal maidservant went with her and Madame Guyon continued to love, worship, pray, and commune with her beloved heavenly Father while in prison. It was stormed in 1789 and later demolished.

After her final release in 1703, Madame Guyon lived exiled from Paris in Blois, a small French village. One of her sons went with her, and for fifteen years she wrote religious poetry and carried on correspondence. She had published several books on spirituality and poetry in 1685. In 1716 she published another book describing how one could grow in the Christian faith. She was visited by many of the leading theologians, priests, and preachers of the day, Roman Catholic and Protestant. Many from England and Scotland came to pay their respects with deep appreciation for her spirituality. Fenelon also kept in touch with her and never wavered in his reverence for and admiration of Madame Guyon. She died in Blois, France, in 1717, at the age of sixty-nine, cared for and accompanied by her faithful son.

Getting Personal

I cannot imagine the difficulties Madame Guyon suffered in prison after having lived as one of the wealthiest of French women. Whenever I had difficulties in my marriage or family life, I thought of her and how she developed such an intimate relationship with God that she was comforted. I tried to emulate her, asking God to enable me to know Him and to pray to Jesus instead of reacting to my circumstances. It helped a great deal. Just remembering Madame Guyon was an encouragement to me.

I also loved learning about Fenelon and his devotion to the education of young women. I greatly valued the education of our three daughters. My former husband and I encouraged all of our children to study as much as they could and to take their education seriously, which they did.

The practice of inner silence known as Quietism reminds me of Mother Teresa, founder of the order of the Missionaries of Charity. Reporters seeking to discover the secrets of her deep personal relationship with God asked her how she prayed. They asked her what words she used when she prayed.

She answered, "Oh, no, I just listen!" They continued to press her to find out what words God said to her. "Oh!" she explained, "He just listens!"[54] Such deep communion with God inspires me to listen more when I pray. I do struggle with prayer at times and try to remind myself to listen to God, not just tell Him my concerns. Madame Guyon inspires me to keep pressing on in prayer.

I had gone home to New Orleans after my divorce and was living with my parents. My siblings thought I was taking advantage of my parents by living with them and caring for them. They believed many things about the situation that were not true. I loved my parents and believed I was honoring them by helping them live the way they wanted to live. I took very good care of them until my father died at age ninety in 2014. He went home to heaven surrounded by family, love, and prayers. Both of my parents had begged me to stay with them to help them and allow them to die at

[54] The source for this quote is from the author's memory, based on a Trinity Broadcasting interview with Mother Theresa.

home and not be put into nursing homes.

I was the sole caregiver for my mother until she was ninety-two, when my siblings decided to put her in a nursing home. This was a very difficult time for me. I was subjected to rejection, insults, and calumny. During this painful time, the example set by Madame Guyon greatly encouraged me. She bore up under the rejection and mistreatment from her family beautifully. She drew close to Jesus Himself and learned to pray constantly. She felt that God had granted her great pleasures in His presence. She constantly looked to Him to provide all the love and acceptance that she could not get from her family. She suffered greatly, becoming more godly, forgiving, and loving. She also was a great example of a Christian praying for, blessing, and doing good to her enemies.

I have translated parts of her books and enjoyed her admonitions to seek God through intense personal prayer. I did not find anything in them objectionable, let alone worthy of imprisonment. I found her very sincere and passionate and consistent.

Let's Talk

1. What do you admire most about Madame Guyon?
2. What Scriptures come to mind when you consider her life?
3. What do you know or believe about the Roman Catholic Church?
4. What do you think was the source of Madame Guyon's strength?
5. Have you ever tried praying Scripture one word at a time?
6. Do you have a deep intimate relationship with Jesus Christ?
7. If you do not, would you like to have one?
8. Do you know how to begin a true and real relationship with Him?
9. How would you have handled the difficult mother-in-law Madame Guyon had? Would you stand up to her? How would you have dealt with the household servants who abused her?

Nine

Marsha Kay Robertson: A Covenant Keeper

Also known as Miss Kay, Marsha Kay Robertson was a cheerleader and a debutante in high school. She began dating Phil Robertson, now the patriarch of the Duck Dynasty, in 1964 when she was fourteen. They married in 1968 and had four children. They now have several grandchildren and great grandchildren.[55]

Miss Kay and the Robertsons are very involved in prison ministry. They have a ministry helping men and women who have just come out of prison become stabilized and build productive lives outside of prison. This is hard and challenging work. The Duck Dynasty has done a great deal of good

---

[55] Much of the info provided on Marsha K. Robertson is taken from an interview with her on the *700 Club* with Pat Robertson in 2012 and from *Miss Kay's Duck Commander Kitchen: Faith Family, and Foodood—Bringing Our Home to Your Table*.

helping inmates rebuild their lives. They help prisoners who have been released find jobs, homes, and churches to attend. They have had many successes. Of course, some released inmates may not make it, but without people like the Robertsons, who not only care but take action, there would be more lives lost.

Thanks to the success of the *Duck Dynasty* television series, Miss Kay's children are now household names. Willie Robertson is probably the most famous of the four. The others are Jules Jeptha Robertson, also known as Jep; Jason Robertson, known as Jase; and Alan Merritt Robertson. Marsha Robertson has written and published a delightful cookbook, *Miss Kay's Duck Commander Kitchen: Faith, Family, and Food, Bringing Our Home to Your Table.*[56]

Kay's husband, Phil, played football in high school, then earned a master's degree in education. Unfortunately, he decided to lease a bar in Arkansas, where he went wild.[57] Kay lived in an apartment with her young sons and prayed for Phil. She was not separated from her husband by her own

---

[56] Kay Robertson, *Miss Kay's Duck Commander Kitchen: Faith, Family, and Food—Bringing Our Home to Your Table* (New York: Howard Books, a division of Simon & Shuster, 2013).
[57] Melissa Barnhart, "'Duck Dynasty' Stars Phil, Miss Kay: How Jesus Christ Saved Their Marriage, Restored Their Family," *Christianpost.com*, May 18, 2013, https://www.christianpost.com/news/duck-dynasty-stars-phil-miss-kay-how-jesus-christ-saved-their-marriage-restored-their-family.html.

will, but the separation was forced upon her. She ended up following the admonitions in 1 Corinthians 7:10–11: "To the married, I give this command (not I, but the Lord): A wife must not separate from her husband. But if she does, she must remain unmarried or else be reconciled to her husband. And a husband must not divorce his wife."

Miss Kay says she was raised more by her grandmother than by her parents. Her grandmother had told her she would someday have to fight for her marriage, but that it would be worth it.

"Fight for your marriage," she had told her. "No matter what people think or what they tell you, your marriage is worth fighting for."

Kay stood for her marriage for ten years while Phil led a violent and dissipated lifestyle. During this time, Miss Kay went to a Bible-believing church where she gave her life to Jesus Christ and was converted to Christianity.

The separation time was very difficult for Miss Kay. Looking back upon his conversion, Phil says, "It's literally what Jesus says, it is like going from darkness to light." The path Miss Kay took by praying for her husband reminds me of the verses in the fifth chapter of James: "Is any one of you in trouble? He should pray. . . . The prayer of a righteous man is powerful and effective" (James 5:13, 16).

When they appeared on *The 700 Club* with Pat Robertson in 2012, the Robertsons were asked,

"What do you think it is that draws people to your family and the values that you share?" The family was on TV constantly, eating dinner together as a family, loving each other, and praying in the name of Jesus. The Robertsons had a lot to say about their family.

Miss Kay talked about Phil Robertson's dark times and how the family endured. She praised the influence her grandmother had had on her. Phil honored Kay and complimented her, giving her great credit for holding the family together. He said that they were a very honest and very happy family. Someone on *The 700 Club* said, "Y'all are so *real!* We can relate to y'all!"

Phil said that when you stay close to the previous generations, it is the best thing in the whole world. He said that America has lost that, and that it is really a sad thing. He said that his family is a pretty fair picture of a godly family in America today.

Phil said that once that disciplined respect for elders is lost, if it's not centered on Jesus, young people don't respect their elders. Once that respect is broken, they won't respect authority at all and everything just breaks down. "And that's what's happened to us (America)," he says, "It's sad."

Miss Kay told one of her sons while their dad was away from God, that the devil was influencing him. She told him that his dad had a good heart

and was a good man, but that the devil was occu-
pying his mind and affecting what he was doing.
So she told her sons that they were not to hate their
dad, but to love and pray for him. They were to
hate Satan and the forces of darkness beyond Satan
that were influencing him.

In answer to Miss Kay's prayers, Phil ultimately gave his life to the Lord Jesus. He sold out to
Jesus 100 percent and became very active in their
church. When Phil came to Christ, one of his sons
said, "The devil ain't in him anymore." Phil started
changing. He turned into a unique and effective
head of a family that became an inspiration for
families all over America.

Korie Robertson, Miss Kay's daughter-in-law,
appearing on *The 700 Club* in 2015, said she was
completely surprised that the television show that
ran for six seasons was so successful. She said she
hoped that other believers would step up and get
into entertainment. She believes America is hun-
gry for wholesome family entertainment and good
role models. She said they did not set out to witness, but their faith is such an important part of
everything they do that it was just naturally woven
into the show. She believes that when the family
prayed together before each meal that America was
thrilled. With six successful seasons, it is believed
to be one of the most watched reality shows of its
time.

Getting Personal

One of the reasons I love the Robertsons is that they do prison ministry. I did prison ministry when I lived in Dallas, Texas. I still support a ministry to the women's prison in Gatesville, Texas. I used to go down to Gatesville on a regular basis to encourage the women in prison to follow Jesus and let Him change their lives while they were still incarcerated.

In New Orleans, I became involved with the Bill Glass Ministries (also a prison ministry) and loved Rick and Alice Bair, who were the organizers and backers of the crusade there. Bill Glass uses celebrities, football players, musicians, gymnasts, and other performers to go into the prisons to entertain the inmates and preach the gospel. Most prison ministries are small Bible studies, which are excellent but only reach a small percentage of the prison population. Bill Glass's artists appeal to the entire inmate population. Most prisoners are bored and thrilled to have some good entertainment. The entertainers are so attractive and so effective in presenting the gospel that many of the prisoners give their lives to Christ. Some people think poorly of this as simply "jailhouse conversions," but the follow-up Bible studies and other ministries attest to the fact that many lives are truly changed.

I soon learned that even for those who had made sincere commitments to God, upon release and reentry into the world, often they didn't make it. Chuck Colson's prison ministry found that if the inmates would commit to a group where they would be accountable and supported and attend the meetings of that group, they were much more likely to establish good and honest lives.

While I was living in New Orleans, Louisiana, taking care of my elderly parents, I taught Bible studies at a juvenile detention center. Again, we found that once the teenagers returned to an unsafe home environment, they were less likely to stay on the straight and narrow. They needed what the Robertsons provide in their prison ministry.

Forgiveness must be looked at again. Kay had to forgive Phil for his absence and his behavior during the ten years they were separated.

One of the greatest examples of forgiveness I have seen was the testimony of Eva Core. She and her twin ten-year-old sister had been in the Nazi death camps and were experimented on. Her sister died. Eva began to forgive and achieved total forgiveness over a period of time. She preached that forgiveness is the most self-empowering and healing action we can take. She urged her listeners to never give up on themselves or on their dreams. She said we should keep working on problems and the solution would be found.

Let's Talk

1. What do you know about the *Duck Dynasty* show on TV? What movies have you seen starring any of the Robertsons?
2. What do you know now about the Robertson family that you didn't know before reading this chapter?
3. How do you think Miss Kay was able to wait for Phil and pray for him?
4. What Scriptures come to mind when thinking of Miss Kay?
5. How did God reward her for her faithfulness?
6. What do you admire most about Miss Kay? About Phil Robertson?
7. What other movies or TV programs do you know that help promote good values?

Ten

Sonya Carson:
Raising Ben Carson

onya Carson, struggling to raise her two young sons, was horrified to discover that the husband she had married, trusted, and had borne two sons to, had another family. He had lied to her about his situation and had lost interest in the children they had had together, Ben and his brother, Curtis, as they grew older. Devastated, she decided to divorce him and to go live with her sister in Boston. Her son Ben Carson was eight years old at the time.[58]

Ben Carson's mother, Sonya Carson, was a devoted Christian who was determined that her sons would receive excellent educations. She insisted that Ben and his brother, Curtis, both read and report on two books each week. They would choose

---

[58] Sonya Carson has personally given her permission for the author to use Sonya's information.

a book, read it, and hand the book report in to her. Once she made it clear that this was a discipline that she was going to enforce, they made the trip to the local library almost every day, racing to see who could get there first.

Sonya Carson supported her young sons by cleaning houses. She also cared for other people's children and held down different jobs to keep the family afloat. They lived in an environment that did not encourage achievement, and she made sure that her sons would be different. Candy Carson, Ben's wife, tells us that Sonya later sewed her lacy satin wedding dress and veil.[59] She also made pottery and made sure her sons had musical training in their early years. She was not only dedicated but very talented and had diverse interests.

After the divorce, Sonya raised the children herself. Ben says that he had wanted to be a physician since he was eight years old. His discipline in doing his homework helped prepare him for his career. Early in his life he decided that he wanted to be the best at anything he attempted. This drive to do his best stood him in good stead for later academics.

Sonya wisely encouraged her sons to love music. She arranged for them to share an instrument, a clarinet. They were in different grades and their band classes met at different times so they could

[59] Candy Carson, *A Doctor in the House* (New York: Sentinel Press, 2016), 15.

share the one instrument. She was very frugal.[60] Their love of music continued throughout their lives. Ben and his wife, Candy, have participated in many church choirs during their marriage.

Sonya was a devout Christian woman of strong character. She was one of twenty-four children and was married when she was just thirteen. Her husband, Robert Carson, was fifteen years older than she was and rescued her from a home life of poverty and abuse. She had lived in foster homes. Her husband was attentive until they had children and then she says he became neglectful and secretive. When Ben was eight and his brother, Curtis, was ten, the marriage ended in divorce. Sonya left their home town of Detroit and moved to Boston as a single mother to live with her sister and her husband. She raised Ben and Curtis on her own. Sometimes she worked three jobs to support the family.

Sonya says she turned to God to be her best friend and told Him she didn't have any other friends so He would have to be her best friend. Her faith in God helped her through hard times. Her life motto was, "Learn to do your best and God will do the rest." Ben Carson later in life attributed his success to Sonya. "Just thinking about her and her life encourages me and gives me the faith and hope to go on," he has said.

Sonya earned her GED in 1969 and was award-

---

[60] Carson, *A Doctor in the House*, 71.

ed an honorary doctorate in 1986. She passed on to her sons a love of learning and a strong work ethic.[61] She made them do their homework. Ben Carson did very well in school and ended up with a scholarship to Yale University. He went to the University of Michigan Medical School, a prestigious and outstanding medical school. Then he was accepted to a much sought-after residency at Johns Hopkins Hospital. Johns Hopkins is a top-ranked hospital famous for its cutting-edge research and excellent care. Ben also trained in Australia, came back to America, and became a very experienced and excellent brain surgeon. At John's Hopkins he pioneered brain surgeries and separated difficult Siamese twins who were joined at the head.

The life of Ben Carson's mother proves that from the most deprived and negative environment, children can be brought up to be successful and achieve great things. Curtis and Ben both went on to become successful. When Ben and his wife, Candy, built their first house, they included an in-law suite for Sonya with a kiln for her ceramics.[62] She lived with them for years and traveled with them when Ben went to speak to various groups.

Sonya helped Ben and Candy Carson raise their three sons and she was a great comfort to the whole family. They loved her and made her an important part of the family. One night when

[61] Carson, *A Doctor in the House*, p. 118.
[62] Carson, *A Doctor in the House*, 101.

their son Rhoeyce had a severe asthma attack, Ben and Candy took him to an emergency room while Sonya stayed home with her other two grandsons, Murray and BJ.[63]

Ben spoke up for issues he believed in and gained great respect and the devotion of the American people. He ran for president in 2016 and handled himself admirably. It is doubtful if Ben Carson could have achieved all that he did if his mother had not disciplined and trained him early in life. Her love and dedication surely were a foundation for his own faith and success. Sonya will always be remembered as one of the best mothers in America!

Getting Personal

I loved Sonya's emphasis on reading. When our children were starting elementary school, my husband took away the TV for months, and we took them to the local library frequently. Our son warned his father that he was going to have to pay a lot of library fines. His father was thrilled with the prospect, but as I remember, we didn't pay any fines. The children read voraciously, and it was a great summer of reading.

Being a mother who wanted the best for her children, I can identify with Sonya Carson. I tried to make my children do their homework. I home-schooled them when that looked like the best way

---

[63] Carson, *A Doctor in the House*, 105.

to motivate and educate them. We encouraged our oldest daughter to study abroad when the opportunity presented itself, and she studied in England at Kingston University. She was able to work as an intern in Vienna, Austria, and studied German. It was in Vienna that she met her wonderful husband. Our middle daughter spent two years in Africa on the Mercy Ships as a missionary registered nurse. As a single Christian young woman at the time of this writing, she still takes medical mission trips around the world.

Our son studied hard and went to law school, and our youngest daughter has degrees in physics and electrical engineering. We spent years praying for, encouraging, and supporting our children while they got their educations. I know that Sonya sacrificed a great deal for her sons, and I admire her.

When I go through hard times and feel like I don't have enough friends, her story greatly encourages me. I like the idea of telling God He has to be my best friend now. I believe Sonya was a loving and kind person as well as a disciplined and determined person.

My mother was pregnant with me when my father told her that, as a flight surgeon, he was being sent to Alaska by the Air Force and he would miss my birth. She was living in New Orleans, where they had met and where their families lived. My mother's father was a Missouri Synod Evangelical Lutheran minister. My dad's father was a poet and a southern gentleman. My mother's mother was a godly homemaker and the wife of a minister. My father's mother was a reformer and a crusader who preached the benefits of yogurt to anyone who would listen.

Because my father was in the Air Force, I grew up moving every year in the middle of the school year. I would be stared at as "the new girl" in each new class and I would cry. The next year I would be elected class president and we would move again. Fortunately, we had a fun peer group within the family as I had four brothers and a sister. We were very close as children. I was bossy and thought it was my job to tell the other children what to do. As we grew up, I lost that magical sisterly power.

I had a blessed and happy childhood, which did not prepare me for the heartaches and realities of life in this sinful world. The unspoken philosophy in our family was that if you are good and do your homework the best that you can, everything will be all right. I didn't learn about Satan's attacks and about the troubles life can bring until much later in life.

I was saved as a young child in a Lutheran Sunday school class, singing "Stand Up, Stand Up for Jesus" with all my heart. Just before college I recommitted my life to the Lord and tried to live for Him in Intervarsity Christian Fellowship for the first two years of college. Then I went out of fellowship for several years and couldn't remember Jesus. He called me back to Him in the middle of law school, where my adventures had taken me.

I remember sitting in a law school exam staring at the blackboard, wondering what to write on an exam question. On the board was written the basics of the pamphlet, *The Four Spiritual Laws*, and I remembered Jesus and all the Christian teaching I had learned. I prayed right then and there and the Lord helped me finish the exam. I graduated from law school and passed the Louisiana State Bar Exam. I had a wonderful job after law school, helping elderly clients learn about their legal rights. Then I asked the Lord for a husband, and He gave me a dedicated Christian man.

We had four children, three daughters and a son. We were leaders in the homeschool and pro-life movements. Then Satan attacked, and we ended up in divorce. I believe most divorces are great tragedies and not God's will. After the divorce, I prayed for my former husband and his new wife and worked on forgiveness. There is no doubt in my mind that in heaven we will all hug and kiss and say, "I'm so sorry!"

The trials and troubles I faced that God has delivered me from as He worked His salvation out in my heart are detailed in the chapters in this book.

I hope my story has been an inspiration and an encouragement to you. I want to assure you that God has His own purposes for your suffering and that it will not last forever. On the other side is peace that passes understanding, as well as love and security. Keep on keeping on. Don't give up, and look to God for everything.

I will close this chapter with one of my favorite quotes, "Forgiveness is setting the prisoner free—and discovering that the prisoner is you." –Author unknown

Let's Talk

1. Describe how Sonya was able to change the futures of her sons.
2. From where do you think she got her determination?
3. What Scriptures come to mind when you think of Sonya?
4. What do you know about Ben Carson?
5. Can you share dreams and goals that you have had for your own children?
6. How do you think Sonya felt when she faced so many hardships? Do you think she was ever tempted to give up? What kept her going?
7. What keeps you going when you face hardships? Are you ever tempted to give up?

Eleven

Redemptive Suffering

When we are trying to understand suffering, it is helpful to look at the book of Job in the Bible. According to Job, one cause of suffering can be that God has been bragging about us, about our love for Him. God was bragging about Job to Satan. Satan said, "Let me afflict him and then you will see what is in Job's heart."

Job shows us how to face suffering with a godly perspective. When Job learned that he had lost everything—children, servants, and livestock, the first thing he did was to fall down and worship God. Worship is a choice, and we can choose to worship any time and any place. Job said, "Naked I came from my mother's womb, and naked I will depart. The Lord gave and the Lord has taken away; may the name of the Lord be praised" (Job 1:21).

Job was very open and dramatic in his grief.

He tore his clothes and shaved his head, as was customary in his culture. He grieved openly and let his friends see his pain. He was very vocal. It is healthy to share our grief with true friends and to let them comfort us. Hopefully, our friends are not like Job's friends, who insisted that he was being punished for some wrongdoing. We hope that our friends can comfort us with the comfort with which they have been comforted by God.

The Bible tells us that Job was a righteous, godly, holy man. He was also very rich and had been blessed with many children. After all his troubles, even being afflicted by sores from head to toe, the Bible says that Job did not sin in what he said. He said, "Shall we accept good from God and not trouble?" (Job 2:10).

It is very comforting to read the whole book of Job, as he defends himself before his friends. He expresses his pain and grief in very strong terms. When God finally heals him, God does not tell him why he has had to suffer, but basically says, "I am God and you are not."

As we seek God in our suffering, we find hope. "Though He slay me, yet will I hope in Him" (Job 13:15). We also find wisdom. "The fear of the Lord, that is wisdom, and to shun evil is understanding" (Job 28:28). Job also found the assurance of eternal life. "I know that my Redeemer lives, and that in the end He will stand upon the earth. And after my skin has been destroyed, yet in my flesh I will see God. I myself will see Him with my own eyes, I and not another. How my heart yearns within me!" And here we have the key to redemptive suffering. We can face anything if God is our everything.

The Bible says in the epistle of James that trials are sent to test our faith. Rick Warren said in his excellent book *The Purpose Driven Life* that life itself is a test.[64] God wants to see if we will honor and obey Him in difficult circumstances. He also wants to teach us that man does not live by bread alone. God wants to test and strengthen our faith and He uses trials to do this. Whether God just allows trials or actually causes them, God uses them to test our faith. Let us just trust Scripture, which tells us that they are sent to test our faith. We can ask God what we can learn in these trials so that we do not waste our suffering.

It is very important to pray and to stay close to God during our trials. We should make sure we are being obedient to God in all areas we are aware of. The first chapter of James tells us that we can ask God for wisdom, and that includes asking for wisdom about how to go through trials. We grow spiritually during the hard times more than in the easy times.

One result of asking for wisdom should be the realization of anything we are doing or have done

[64] Rick Warren, *The Purpose Driven Life* (Grand Rapids, Michigan: Zondervan, 2002), 42.

that may have caused our suffering. If we have gossiped and slandered a friend and that friend finds out, causing us to suffer rejection, we must be aware of this so that we can correct our behavior. If our own sins have caused us to suffer, our trials can give the Holy Spirit the opportunity to reveal to us what we need to repent of and what behaviors we need to change.

God may be teaching us wisdom by letting us go through difficult times. If the suffering *is* a result of our own sin, God may let us suffer the consequences so that we can learn wisdom. Those who have gone through suffering and have come out on the other side believe that God then uses them to comfort and strengthen others who face similar situations. God says in His Word in 2 Corinthians that we are to comfort those who need comforting with the comfort with which we have been comforted.

As covered in other chapters, when our suffering is caused by the behavior of other people, total forgiveness results in the easing of the pain of rejection, divorce, gossip, slander, and many other wrongs. I have found that the greatest relief from this kind of suffering comes from praying for enemies or those who have hurt us. We can do this out of obedience to Jesus, and it is nearly miraculous in its healing power.

Ephesians 5:20 tells us to give thanks in everything. Merlin Carothers taught that we should praise and thank God *for* everything. Merlin takes our focus off of the problem and puts the focus on God, who is the ultimate deliverer and problem solver. I have found these practices a shortcut to problem solving. Spending our time thanking God for anything and everything we can think of keeps us from excessive worrying about the problem. Another reason that we can thank God in every situation is again from the principles in the eighth chapter of Romans where we are told that in everything God works for the good of those who love Him and are called according to His purposes. This means that no matter how bad the situation is, if we wait long enough, go through the trial trusting Him, and look for His work, He will bring good out of it.

In 2011, I was visiting First Baptist Church in New Orleans. The church had been flooded in Hurricane Katrina. The pastor asked God why He lets such terrible tragedies happen. Most of this pastor's congregation had to leave New Orleans due to the flooding. The pastor himself had to go sleep on a couch in his daughter's home on the Gulf Coast and wear borrowed clothes. The pastor said that God led him to Deuteronomy 8 in the Bible.

I am not going to quote it here because you would best benefit from going and reading the whole chapter yourself. But I will summarize what it teaches us. God often sends or allows trials in order to humble us, to test us, and to find out what is in our hearts. He wants to know whether or not we will obey Him when times are tough. He let the Israelites hunger and thirst in the wilderness so that He could feed them manna and teach them that man does not live by bread alone, but by every word that proceeds from the mouth of God. God tested the Israelites in the wilderness, but He was leading them to a promised land flowing with milk and honey. He says in Deuteronomy 8 that as a man disciplines his son, out of love, so God disciplines us. God disciplined the Israelites for complaining and for not trusting Him enough to enter the promised land the first time.

It is important to ask God for wisdom when we are going through trials because He might be disciplining us for our good. It is the job of the Holy Spirit to convict us of wrongdoing and to help us to change. But remember, not all trials occur because of our sins or our mistakes. Job suffered partly because God had been bragging about how wonderful he was to Satan. Job is a great book to read when we or those we love are going through trials because it puts everything in the eternal perspective.

My prayer for us is that Jesus Himself will strengthen and comfort us as we face our tribulations and endure suffering. In this fallen and sinful world, we will all suffer in some way. It is good to remind ourselves that this world is not the end. God has promised those of us who have put our trust in His Son Jesus Christ that we will be in heaven with Him. In heaven there will be no more tears, pain, sin, or sorrow. We will all love one another and love God. We will be like Jesus was when He was resurrected from the dead. He ate fish, cooked, passed through walls, appeared and disappeared, and could make Himself unrecognizable. This is our ultimate end and if we have endured suffering in a godly and constructive way on earth, our character may be stronger in heaven and our enjoyment greater. We are promised that if we endure suffering, God will reward us. The study of heaven and all of its wonders is a good antidote for suffering. So is helping other people, praying, reading Scripture, journaling, exercising, and taking a long hot bath.

One greatly hoped-for result of suffering is that we get to know God better. As God walks with us through our miseries and pain, we do get to know how compassionate, kind, loving, and personal He is. We can draw closer to Christ as we take up our cross and follow Him. If we suffer from anxiety and worry, we can turn to Him in prayer and petition, thanking Him for everything we can think of to thank Him for. May God bless us as we honor Him in all that we do. May we look to Him for comfort and strength as we go through whatever comes our way in this world. May God bless and comfort us as we overcome our trials and tribulations, giving praise and glory to Him alone.

Bibliography

Augustine. *Confessions*, trans. F. J. Sheed. New York: Sheed and Ward, 1943.

Barnhart, Melissa. "*Duck Dynasty* Stars Phil, Miss Kay: How Jesus Christ Saved Their Marriage, Restored Their Family." *Christianpost.com*, May 18, 2013. https://www.christianpost.com/news/duck-dynasty-stars-phil-miss-kay-how-jesus-christ-saved-their-marriage-restored-their-family.html.

Benedict XVI. *Church Fathers from Clement of Rome to Augustine.* San Francisco: Ignatius Press, 2008.

Carothers, Merlin R. *Prison to Praise*. Escondido, California, 1970.

Carson, Candy. *A Doctor in the House.* New York: Sentinel Press, 2016.

de Sales, Francis. *Introduction to the Devout Life.* New York: Harper & Row, 1966.

Elliot, Elisabeth. *Discipline, the Glad Surrender.* Grand Rapids, Michigan: Revell, 1982.

Elliot, Elisabeth. *Passion and Purity.* Old Tappan, New Jersey: Power Books, Fleming H. Revell Company, 1984.

Falbo, Giovanni. *Saint Monica: The Power of a Mother's Love.* Boston: Pauline Books and Media, 2007.

Guyon, Madame Jeanne. *A Short and Easy Method of Prayer.* Amazon Digital Services, 2010.

Guyon, Madame Jeanne. *Christian and Spiritual Letters on Various Subjects Regarding the Interior Life of the Spirit and the Christian Life.* London, MD-CCLLXVII.

Johnson, Barbara. *Stick a Geranium in Your Hat and Be Happy!* Nashville: W Publishing Group, a division of Thomas Nelson Inc., 2004.

Johnson, Barbara. *I'm So Glad You Told Me What I Didn't Wanna Hear.* Dallas: Word Publishing, 1996.

Morgan, Robert. *The Red Sea Rules.* Nashville: W Publishing Group, a division of Thomas Nelson Inc., 2014.

Robertson, Kay. *Miss Kay's Duck Commander Kitchen: Faith, Family, and Food, Bringing Our Home to Your Table.* New York: Howard Books, a division of Simon & Shuster, 2013.

Smith, Hannah Whitall. *The Christian's Secret of a Happy Life.* Grand Rapids: Revell, a division of Baker Publishing Group, 1952.

Smith, Hannah Whitall. *Religious Fanaticism: Extracts from the papers of Hannah Whitall Smith.* New York: AMS Press, 1976.

Vulliamy, C. E. *John Wesley.* Westwood, New Jersey: Barbour and Company Inc., 1985.

Wurmbrand, Sabina. *The Pastor's Wife.* Bartlesville, Oklahoma: Living Sacrifice Book Company, 1970.

Order Information

To order additional copies of this book, please visit
www.redemption-press.com.
Also available on Amazon.com and
BarnesandNoble.com
or by calling toll-free 1-844-2REDEEM.